# FHM
## PRESENTS THE BEST OF
## BAR-ROOM JOKES

CARLTON
BOOKS

## The Ordeal of Fruit

Two men shipwrecked on an island are captured by cannibals. The chief informs them the only way to avoid becoming dinner is to undergo the 'Ordeal of Fruit'. The men accept at once, and the chief sends them into the jungle to collect 100 pieces of fruit and bring them back to him.
The first man comes back with 100 grapes. The chief says that if he can shove all the grapes up his arse without giggling then he will be free. But no sooner has the first grape reached his butt than the man bursts out laughing.
'What's so funny?' the chief asks. 'Don't you realize we're going to kill you now?'
'I'm sorry,' the sailor replies. 'It's just that my friend is collecting pineapples.'

## The Amish go to town

An Amish boy and his father rode into town to visit a new shopping mall. All that they saw had them reeling in amazement, but the one thing that really caught their eye was a pair of shiny 'walls' that could slide open and close effortlessly shut again. The boy looked at his father and asked, 'What is this thing, father?'
Having never seen an elevator before, the old man responded:
'Son, I have never seen anything like this in my life. I don't know what it is.'
At that moment, a fat lady in a wheelchair rolled up to the moving walls and pressed a button. The walls opened and the lady moved between them into a small room. The walls then closed, and the boy and his father watched in awe as a series of semi-circular numbers above the walls lit up sequentially. They continued to stare as the numbers lit in reverse order. Finally the walls opened again and a gorgeous, voluptuous blonde woman stepped out.
Without taking his eyes off the young woman, the father said quietly:
'Son, go get your mother ...'

## Drunk driving (i)

A man is driving happily along when he is pulled over by the police.
The copper approaches him and politely asks, 'Have you been drinking, sir?'
'Why?' snorts the man. 'Is there a fat bird in my car?'

## A fisherman's mistake

A fisherman is sorting through his catch on the edge of a lake when a man sprints up to him, obviously in some distress.

'Help me please,' he gasps. 'My wife is drowning and I can't swim.' He points out to a distant figure, splashing around pathetically 100 m from the shore. 'Please save her. I'll give you a hundred quid if you do.'

Nodding, the fisherman dives into the water. In a few powerful strokes, he reached the woman, puts his arm around her, and swims back to shore. Depositing her at the feet of the man, he looks up at him.

'Okay,' he says, regaining his breath, 'where's my hundred?'

The man frowns back at him. 'Look,' he says. 'When I saw her going down for the third time, I thought it was my wife. But this is my mother-in-law.'

The fisherman reached into his pocket. 'Just my luck,' he says. 'How much do I owe you?'

## The butcher's haircut

A man walks into a butcher's. 'Excuse me,' he asks, 'Have you got a sheep's head?'

'No,' says the butcher. 'It's the way I brush my hair.'

## Never gamble with a chemist

This deaf mute strolls into a chemist's shop to buy a packet of condoms. Unfortunately, the mute cannot see any of his required brand on the shelves, and the chemist, unable to decipher sign language, fails to understand what the man wants.

Frustrated, the deaf mute decides to take drastic action: he unzips his trousers and drops his cock on the counter, before placing a £5 note next to it. Nodding, the chemist unzips his own trousers, performs the same manoeuvres as the mute, then picks up both notes and stuffs them in his pocket.

Exasperated, the deaf mute begins to curse the chemist with a wild gesturing of his arms 'Sorry,' the chemist says, shrugging his shoulders. 'But if you can't afford to lose, you shouldn't gamble.'

# He said she'd be sorry ...

From the day of their wedding, Sarah has been nagging her husband about his past.

'Come on, tell me,' she asks again, 'how many women have you slept with?'

'Honey, ' he says, 'if I told you, you'd just get angry.'

'No, I promise I won't,' she begs.

'Well, If you insist. Let's see. One ... two ... three ... four ... you ... six ... seven ...'

# Urinary graphology

Prince Charles arrives home to find 'Charles is a wanker' written in the snow. He says to his detective:

'This seems to be written in urine. Do some tests and find out who did it.'

Later that day, the detective returns from the lab.

'Bad news, I'm afraid, sir. The urine is Will Carling's.'

'Why is that bad?'

'Well, sir, the handwriting is Princess Diana's.'

# We love Fergie really

What do you get when you cross Fergie with a gorilla?

Don't know. There's only so much you can force a gorilla to do.

# The accommodating wife

A woman complains to her friend that her husband is losing interest in sex, and he prefers nights out with the lads to the joys of copulation. Her friend tells her that to win his love she must make more effort. She advises her to cook a slap-up meal and them send him drinking with his pals down the pub. When he returns she must be dressed in her naughtiest lingerie and look her most beautiful.

The following evening, she does exactly as instructed and is dressed to kill by the time her husband returns. When he sees her lying on the bed in all her gear, he tells to stand up and take it all off. He then tells her to do a handstand against the bathroom mirror and open her legs. This excites the woman immensely, as her husband has never been this erotic before. She does as instructed, and then he puts his face between her legs, faces the mirror and says, 'No, no ... Maybe the lads are right. A beard wouldn't suit me.'

## Mistaken diagnosis

A woman is lying in the road after being run over. The driver of the vehicle that knocked her down comes to her help. 'Are you all right, love?' he asks.

'You're just a blur,' she says. 'So my sight is clearly affected.'

Very concerned, the driver leans over the woman in order to test her eyesight. 'How many fingers have I got up?' he asks her.

'Oh shit!' she replies. 'I must be paralysed from the waist down as well.'

## Booby prize

After a woman meets a man in a bar, they talk and end up leaving together. They get back to his flat, and as he's showing her around, she notices that his bedroom is completely packed with teddy bears. Hundreds of them – all arranged in size, from the smallest on the shelves along the floor, to the huge Daddy bears on the very top shelf.

Surprised, the woman still decides not to mention this to him. After an intense night of passion, as they are lying there together in the afterglow, the woman rolls over and asks, smiling, 'Well, how was it?'

'Well,' says the man, frowning. 'You can have any prize from the bottom shelf.'

# Overheard ... in a London cab

**A butter boy:** A driver who has only recently earned the right to call himself a 'cabbie'.

**The gasworks:** The place you and I would normally call the Houses of Parliament.

**Mush:** An owner/driver.

**A bilk:** One of the minority who spoil things for everyone by running off without paying.

**A legal:** Tight-fisted type who finds tipping impossible.

**Droshki:** Sounds foreign and exotic, but really it's just a black cab.

**Hair dryer:** Jocular description for the hated hand-held radar speed device.

**Bowler hat:** A city gent.

**The Oil Rig:** The Lloyd's Building in the City of London.

**The Wedding Cake:** London's Queen Victoria memorial.

**Icory:** Heaven knows why, but it's the taxi meter.

**Scab:** Even more reprehensible than a 'bilk', this lowly creature is a mini-cab driver.

**A roader:** A long job.

**A shit:** A short job.

**A wrong'un:** Similar to a 'shit' – especially unwelcome from fares at airports.

## All fingers and thumbs

While cutting wood in his workshop, Jim the carpenter slips and manages to slice all his fingers off on his powerful electric saw. He screams and runs out of the workshop, sprinting in considerable pain to the nearest hospital. After he has been waiting half an hour, a nurse emerges.

'I'm sorry, sir,' she says, 'but without your fingers, we can't do anything except stop the bleeding. Go back and get our fingers so we can sew them back on.'

Nodding forlornly, Jim wanders out of casualty. An hour later, he returns.

'Did you recover your fingers, sir?' asks the nurse.

'No,' he replied. 'I couldn't pick them up off the floor.'

## Is that a frog in your pocket ...?

A man surveys the women in a nightclub, picks out the most attractive, and takes a seat next to her at the bar. He uses all his best lines, but gets nowhere. Finally, he reaches into his pocket, takes out a small box, and pulls a frog out of it.

'Cute,' says the woman. 'Is that a pet?'

The man smiled. 'Yes, and he's good at doing tricks too.'

'Like what?'

'He eats pussy. Come back to my place and I'll prove it to you ...'

Once in the bedroom, the girl strips off and puts the frog between her legs. The frog doesn't move. After a couple of minutes the woman looks at the immobile frog, and finally demands, 'Well?'

The man shakes his head sorrowfully, picks up the frog, and says, 'Okay, you idiot, I'm only going to show you one more time.'

## The power of drugs

Enid sat at her husband's hospital bedside, watching him slowly regain consciousness as the effects of a particularly powerful anaesthetic wore off. Slowly the man's eyes fluttered open, and, seeing his wife's anxious face looming over him, he murmured, 'You're beautiful.'

An hour later the man's eyes once again opened, and he said, 'You look nice.'

'What happened to beautiful, then?' Enid enquired.

'The drugs are wearing off,' came the frail reply.

## The flute player

While out on a hunting expedition, a man is climbing over a fallen tree when his shotgun goes off, hitting him straight in the groin.

Rushed to hospital, he awakes from the anaesthetic to find the surgeon has done a marvellous job repairing his damaged member. As he dresses to go home, the surgeon wanders over and hands him a business card.

'This is my brother's card. I'll make an appointment for you to see him.'

The guy is shocked. 'But it says here that he's a professional flute player,' he says. 'How can he help me?'

The doctor smiles. 'Well,' he says, 'he's going to show you where to put your fingers so you don't piss in your eye.'

## He's armless

A man with no arms or legs is sunbathing on the beach. He is approached by three beautiful young women who take pity on him. The first says to him, 'Have you ever been hugged?'
The man shakes his head, and she leans down and gives him a big hug.
The second says to him, 'Have you ever been kissed?'
He shakes his head. She kisses him.
Rather abruptly, the third girl asks, 'Have you ever been fucked?'
'No', says the man, his eyes lighting up.
'Well, you are now. The tide's coming in.'

# Knickers!

After ten loyal years working at the local factory, Nigel and Trevor were laid off, so first thing Monday morning they made their way to the DSS. When asked his occupation, Nigel said, 'I'm a panty stitcher. I sew the elastic into cotton knickers.'

The clerk looked up 'panty stitcher' and, finding it to be classed as unskilled labour, gave Nigel £100 a week benefit money.

Trevor then approached the counter and explained that he was a diesel fitter. As diesel fitting was considered to be a skilled occupation, Trevor was awarded £200 a week.

When Nigel learned how much his friend was being given he was furious, and went storming up to the clerk, demanding to know why his mate was collecting double his own pay.

'It says on my list that diesel fitters are an intrinsic part of the skilled labour force,' explained the clerk, patiently.

'What skill?' screamed Nigel. 'I sew in the elastic, he pulls the knickers on and says, "Yup – diesel fitter!"'

# A medical request

A senior lecturer at a London medical college is rather surprised one afternoon when one of his most promising students breaks through the door in a clear state of distress. Sitting the lad down, the kindly old-timer waits for him to compose himself before asking, 'What on earth is the matter?'

'I can't take it anymore, doc,' wails the distressed student. 'I need to find somewhere else to live!'

'But our student digs are the best in the land,' protests the lecturer.

'No, doctor – it's this new policy of mixed living quarters. Every night when I'm trying to study, I have to push away beautiful young nurses, who have come in drunk from a night on the town and are hungry for sex.'

'I see,' says the quack. 'So how do you think I can help?'

'Oh doc,' says the desperate young man, quietly. 'You're going to have to break my arms.'

## The Legion take anyone

A captain in the Foreign Legion was transferred to a desert outpost. On his first day there he noticed a very old, seedy-looking camel tied up at the back of the barracks. He asked his sergeant what this animal was for.

The sergeant replied, 'Well, sir, we're a fair distance from anywhere, and the men have natural sexual urges, so when they do, uh, we have the camel.'

The captain thinks about this, and says, 'Well, if it's good for morale, then I suppose it's all right with me.'

After he has been at the fort for about six months, the captain became very frustrated himself. Finally he could stand it no longer and so he told his sergeant, 'Bring in the camel!'

The sarge shrugged his shoulders and led the camel into the captain's quarters. The captain then got a footstool and began to have vigorous sex with the camel. As he stepped down, satisfied, and was buttoning his pants up, he asked the sergeant, 'Is that how the enlisted men do it?'

The sergeant replied, 'Well, no sir, they usually just use it to ride to the brothel in town.'

## Overheard ... in the Army

**X'd:** Annoyed. From 'cross'. Hence 'Triple X'd' – even crosser.

**On scotches:** Walking. Lord only knows why.

**Comics:** Not the Beano, not Morecambe and Wise, but maps.

**Muzzy:** As a newt.

**Twang your wire:** Solitary sexual entertainment.

**A wet weekend:** Sex (on leave) with a partner who is menstruating.

**Snafu:** Yankee WWII acronym – 'Situation normal, all fucked up'.

**Load of reg:** Bollocks. From 'regimental', or a stickler for discipline.

**Honey:** Unappetizing combination of shit and piss, familiar to latrine cleaners.

**To have a shellfish on the beach:** To have a crab scuttle across your loins.

**Gum-bumper:** A sergeant prone to shouting, whose gums, presumably, bump together constantly.

**On a 48:** Forty-eight hours of weekend leave.

**Film for your brownie:** Izal and Andrex – a double bill of great 'films'.

## The tell-tale fingers

'I'm baffled by your yellow penis,' the doctor told his patient. 'Does anyone else in your family have this condition?'

The concerned fellow shook his head.

'Do you handle any chemicals at work?'

'I don't work. I'm unemployed.'

Well, what do you do all day?'

'Oh, I mostly sit around watching porno movies, eating Quavers.'

## Mistaken identity

Two Irishmen are walking through Calcutta when an old woman wanders past.

'Hey, Seamus,' one says. 'I think that's Mother Teresa.'

'Rubbish,' says the other.

'I'm telling you it was.'

To settle the argument, they approach the lady and ask her.

'Are you Mother Teresa?'

The old woman eyes them scornfully.

'Piss off, you perverts,' she hisses.

'Jeez,' Seamus says, watching her disappear into the crowd. 'Now we'll never know.'

## Not for sale in Scotland

Two Scotsmen are walking down a country lane.

'Och, Duncan,' says Jimmy all of a sudden, 'I dinnae half need a shit.'

'Well, just go behind a bush and do it, then,' replies his mate.

So Jimmy goes behind a bush, and after a while he shouts, 'Have you got any paper?'

To which Duncan replies, 'Och, don't be such a tight bastard. Leave it.'

## What a wanker

Worried about his failing eyesight, a man goes to his optician – who tells him he must stop masturbating.

'Why?' asks the man, worriedly, 'Am I going blind?'

'No, your eyesight is fine,' says the optician, 'But it upsets the other patients in the waiting room.'

## Saving the species

There's a very rare breed of orang-utan, and one of the few left is Daisy, who lives in a zoo. The problem is that Daisy is getting older and her fertility rate is dropping. Scientists in the field can't find a suitable mate for Daisy – but suddenly a report comes out which proves that, for the first time, man can mate with orang-utan.

But who would ever attempt to impregnate a fully grown ape? Well, who better than Paddy? For 17 years, he has been Daisy's zookeeper and if any man has built a bond of trust with her, then it's him. So the scientists call him in and put the proposal to him.

They say, 'Look, Paddy, we know Daisy's really close to you.'

'She's like a partner to me,' Paddy agrees.

'Well, we need someone to mate with the orang-utan and reproduce the species. Time is running out, and we think you're the guy to carry it off.'

Paddy thinks about this for a minute, then says, 'I understand what you're saying, but I'm not interested.'

So they say, 'Look, Paddy, it's a £500 deal and there's a cloak of secrecy wrapped around it. Believe us, it's for Daisy's benefit and the continuation of the species. That's why we're asking you.'

Paddy says, 'Okay. I understand, but let me sleep on it and I'll let you know tomorrow.'

Next day, all the boffins are sitting there. Paddy comes in, very emotional, and says, tears welling in his eyes, 'I'm going to do it, but there are three conditions. One: no kissing on the lips, because it's too intimate.'
The scientists agree.

Paddy continues, 'Two: any child born of this project will be a strict Catholic.'
The scientists say it's no problem.

'And three,' says Paddy, 'you'll need to give me at least a week to get the £500 together.'

## Ask a stupid question ...

At 7am, a lone wife hears a key in the front door. She wanders down, bleary eyed, to find her husband in the kitchen – drunk, with ruffled hair and lipstick on his collar.

'I assume,' she snarls, 'that there is a very good reason for you to come waltzing in here at seven in the morning?'

'There is,' he replies. 'Breakfast.'

## It's all in the phrasing

An Essex girl is out driving one day when her car skids at a roundabout and hits the car in front. As she's injured, an ambulance is called and a paramedic quickly arrives. 'What's your name, love?' he asks.

'Sharon', she replies.

Looking around, the medic sees there's a lot of blood.

'Sharon', he asks, 'where are you bleeding from?'

'Romford', she replies.

## Spelling test

An Irish family are watching television, when the father shouts, 'Bridget! Close your legs! The k-i-d-s can see your cunt.'

## Drunk driving (ii)

While patrolling country lanes around his local village, a young policeman notices a car being driven erratically. With a quick burst of the siren he pulls the driver over, and sternly walks up to the car to ask the gentleman whether he's been drinking.

'Oh aye', says the man, quite proudly. 'It's Friday, so a few of the lads and I went straight to the pub after work, and I must have had about six or seven there. Then we went to the bar next door for happy hour, and they were serving these great cocktails for a pound, so I had three or four of those. Then my cousin Mick asked for a lift home – his sister's sick, you see – so I drove him back. Of course, he asked me in, so I had a Murphy's – lovely stuff it is, too – and took a bottle for the road.'

With that, the man reaches into his coat, pulls out a bottle of scotch, waves it at the policeman, and beams happily.

'Sir, would you exit the vehicle immediately for a breathalyser test', the officer says as calmly as he can.

'Why?' asks the man. 'Don't you believe me?'

## Twin controls

Two Siamese twins go on holiday to the same resort in southern France every year. Unsurprisingly, the head waiter recognizes the conjoined brothers, and asks if they keep coming back for the weather.

'Oh no,' replies one of the twins, 'Actually we burn quite easily.'

'Perhaps you are wine connoisseurs, then?' wonders the waiter.

'Again, no,' says the other twin. 'We're both beer drinkers'

'I know!' cries the waiter. 'It must be the fine French food?'

'Actually,' they say, shaking their heads, 'We prefer English fish and chips.'

The waiter is astounded. 'So what makes you come back year after year?'

'Well,' says one twins, pointing to his brother. 'It's the only chance our kid gets to drive.'

## Caught short

A girl takes her new boyfriend back home after the dance. She tells him to be very, very quiet as her parents are asleep upstairs and if they wake up, she would be in big trouble as she's not allowed to bring boys home.

They settle down to business on the sofa, but after a while, he stops and says, 'Where's the toilet, I need to go.'

She says, 'It's next to my parents' bedroom. You can't go there, you might wake them up. Use the sink in the kitchen instead.'

He goes into the kitchen then, after a short while, he pops his head round the door and says to his girlfriend, 'Have you got any paper?'

## Sand trap

Pinocchio complains to his father saying 'Whenever I attempt to make love to a woman, she complains of splinters.' His father shows pity and gives Pinocchio a piece of sandpaper to smooth his knob down whenever he needs to. A few days later during dinner his father asks, 'How are the girls?'

Pinocchio replies, 'Girls? Who needs girls?'

## Chinese takeaway

A man goes to a disco and starts chatting up a very attractive-looking Chinese girl. After a night of cavorting, she asks him back to her place 'for a coffee'. They get to her flat, and she tells him to help himself to a drink while she slips into something more comfortable. Just as he finishes his drink, the sexy Chinese seductress returns wearing only a see-through negligée.

'I am your sex slave!' she says. 'I will do absolutely ANYTHING you want.'

The man can't believe his luck. 'Hmm,' he says, grinning from ear-to-ear. 'I really fancy a 69.'

'Fuck off!' replies the girl. 'I'm not cooking at this time of night.'

## Shhh!

A blonde walks into a library.

'Excuse me – can I have a burger and large fries, please?' she demands.

Tutting, the librarian looks back at her. 'Miss,' he says, 'this is a library.'

The blonde leans over the counter.

'I'm sorry,' she whispers. 'Can I have a burger and large fries, please?'

## The interpretation of dreams

Waking after a long night's sleep, a wife begins recounting her dream to her husband. 'I dreamt I was at an auction for cocks,' she began. 'The long ones went for a tenner, and the meaty ones for £20.'

'How about the ones like mine?' asked her husband.

'Oh, they gave those away,' she replied, grinning slyly.

Miffed, the husband responds: 'Well I had a dream too – where they were auctioning off pussies. The pretty ones cost £1,000 and the little tight ones went for double that.'

'And how much for the ones like mine?' inquired his wife.

The man grinned. 'Oh, that's where they held the auction.'

## Cut!
Did you hear about the shortsighted circumciser? He got the sack.

## At least someone's happy

A doctor walks into his office, where a patient is anxiously awaiting results from a blood test. 'Mr Stirling, I'm not going to mess you around,' the medic announces. 'There's good news and bad news. Which do you want?'

'Give me the bad stuff,' replies the man.

Calmly, the doc says, 'You've got 48 hours to live.'

His patient howls, claws his hair and moans, 'Oh my God, what am I going to do? Surely there must be a cure!'

'Of course not,' says the doctor, gruffly.

'But I thought you said there was some good news,' sobs the man.

'Oh yes, that's right – there is,' replies the quack, cheerfully. 'Remember the beautiful nurse at reception when you came in?'

'Yes,' replies the puzzled patient.

'The blonde with the tight, white uniform?'

'Yeah! With the big tits!' says the patient, brightening up somewhat.

'Well,' says the doctor, leaning over to whisper. 'I'm shagging her.'

## Dispute Down Under

The Australian Prime Minister flies to England for a meeting with the Queen.
Over a cup of tea, the PM brings up his grand new plan for his country.
'Your Majesty, mate,' he begins. 'Can we turn Australia into a kingdom, in
order to increase our role in the global economy?'

The Queen shakes her head and replies, 'One needs a king for a kingdom,
and unfortunately you are most certainly not a king.'

Not to be dissuaded, the politician asks, 'Would it be possible to transform
Australia into an empire, then?'

'No,' replies the Queen. 'For an empire you need an emperor, and you are
most certainly not an emperor.' The PM thinks for a moment and then asks
if it's possible to turn Australia into a principality.

The Queen replies, 'For a principality, you need a prince – and you are not a
prince.' Pausing for a sip of her tea, Her Majesty then adds: 'I don't mean to
appear rude, but having met both you and several other Australians, I think
Australia is perfectly suited as a country.'

## Overheard ... in Australia

**Apple-islander:** A resident of Tasmania.

**Banana bender:** A resident of Queensland.

**Bludger:** A lazy person.

**Comfort station:** A toilet, fittingly.

**Crow-eater:** A resident of Southern Australia.

**Dag:** Pieces of dried sheep shit. Also a handy insult.

**Floater:** A dish consisting of a meat pie immersed in soup.

**Franger:** A condom.

**'G'day, Blue':** A perverse but standard greeting applied to anyone
who possess red or ginger hair.

**Manchester:** Not just a city, but also a pile of laundry.

**One-pot screamer:** A man who can't hold his drink.

**Sand-groper:** A resident of Western Australia.

**Slygrogging:** The practice of drinking after hours.

**Thongs:** Not a piece of dodgy groin-wear popular with the lead singer
from Cameo, but a pair of flip-flops.

**Underground mutton:** A plate of rabbit.

## Transfer of guilt

Liverpool Football Club are on the look out for some new talent and send a scout to Bosnia where they find a fantastic new player and bring him back with them. In his first game, he scores a hat-trick and the fans love him. When he gets home he decides to phone his mum and give her the good news, but when she answers she immediately starts crying.

When he asks what the matter is, she replies, 'Well, this morning your sister was raped by a street gang, then your little brother was savaged by wild dogs while playing football in the street. After that your dad was shot by a sniper and I was mugged and beaten up while shopping.'

The guy is gobsmacked. 'Mum, what can I say? I'm so sorry.'

'Sorry?!' she shouts. 'It's your fault we moved to Liverpool!'

## Overheard ... the boys in blue

**Black rats:** Bubonic plague carriers. Also, traffic police.

**'We had him across the pavement':** We caught chummy in the act of stealing.

**'In the bin':** In prison.

**Dippers:** Funfare-themed term for pickpockets.

**Toms:** Ladies of the night.

**Blaggers:** Armed chummy.

**Woodentops:** Constables on the beat; a kids' TV programme in the Fifties.

**Probbys:** Probationary policemen and women.

**Plonk:** Derogatory term for a female officer. Nothing whatsoever to do with cheap wine.

**Guv'nor:** An Inspector. Used to very good effect by Carter in The Sweeney.

**A producer:** Not a Mel Brooks film, but the order to show all driving documents at your local cop shop.

**Old sweat:** An ageing, run-down police constable.

**Polacc:** An accident involving a police car and a member of the general public.

**To bag someone:** A breathalyser test.

**Stick/peg:** Truncheon.

**To stick someone:** To hit them with the aforementioned wooden implement.

## Open and shut case

After a long marriage and nine children, a woman's husband dies. Devastated, she nevertheless remarries and has seven more children – before her second husband passes away. Undaunted, she marries for a third time – and has another six children before finally kicking the bucket herself.

At her funeral, the vicar stands next to her coffin and prays for her soul. 'Oh Lord,' says the preacher, 'Protect this woman, who fulfilled your commandment to go forth and multiply. And we thank you, Lord, that they're finally together.'

Leaning over to his neighbour, one of the mourners asks, 'Do you think he means her first, second or third husband?'

The other mourner frowns. 'I think,' he replies, 'that he means her legs.'

## Lucky dog

Three guys are comparing their drunkenness from the night before. The first guy says, 'I was so drunk I don't even know how I got home ... I just woke up in my bed in a pool of sweat.'

'Oh yeah?' brags the second guy. 'I was so wasted I took home a strange woman and was having sex with her when my wife walked in.'

'That's nothing,' says the third guy. 'I was so pissed I was blowing chunks all night.'

'Big deal,' scoff the other two.

The third guy says, 'I don't think you understand – Chunks is the name of my dog.'

## Countdown

After months of ill-health, a man goes to his doctor for a complete check-up. Afterward, the doctor comes out with the results.

'I'm afraid I have some very bad news,' says the physician. 'You're dying, and you don't have much time left.'

'Oh, that's terrible!' says the man. 'How long have I got?'

'Ten,' the doctor replies, shaking his head.

'Ten?' the man asks. 'Ten what? Months? Weeks? What do you mean?'

The doctor looks at him sadly. 'Nine ...'

## Dearth of a princess

Princess Diana and the Queen are being driven around the grounds of Balmoral, when the Land Rover is stopped by a robber. He tells the Queen to wind down her window and hand over all her money.

'I'm the richest woman in the world,' replies the Queen. 'I have no need for money.'

So the robber turns to Diana and demands she hands over all her jewellery.

'I'm the most beautiful woman in the world,' replies Di. 'I have no need for jewellery.'

The robber decides to cut his losses and so steals the Land Rover instead.

When he's gone, the Queen asks Diana where she hid all her jewellery.

'Well,' says Diana, 'when I saw him approaching, I stuffed it all up my fanny. Why, what did you do with all the money you were carrying?'

'Same thing,' says the Queen. 'When I saw him approaching, I stuffed all the cash up my fanny.'

'It's a pity Fergie wasn't here,' says Diana. 'Otherwise we could have saved the Land Rover as well.'


## Size does matter

Three men are marooned on a desert island desperately seeking a way to get off. A cannibal approaches them and flops his penis out. 'If the length of your three penises put together is as big as mine, then I'll show you a way to get off the island,' he says. 'But otherwise you'll be killed and eaten.'

The native's love muscle was a staggering 20 inches. The first man got his out, and it was 10 inches. The second man then produced a 9-inch knob. Realizing they only needed 1 inch to go, the first two men were quietly confident. The third got his penis out, and it was only 1 inch long.

After some tense calculations, the native says, 'Okay, you've equalled the length of my penis. I have a boat which you can use to escape.'

While sailing away on the boat, the first man says to the other two, 'You're lucky I've got a 10-inch penis.'

And the second says, 'You're lucky I've got a 9-inch penis.'

To which the third man replies, 'And you're lucky I had an erection.'

# Happy meal?

One cold winter evening, an elderly couple wander into a fast-food restaurant. As the young families look on, the old gent walks up to the counter, orders a meal and then pays. Taking a seat next to his wife, he slowly unwraps the plain burger and cuts it in two – placing one half in front of his beloved. Then, he carefully divides the fries into two piles: one for him, one for her.

As the man takes a few bites of hamburger, the crowd began to get restless – this is obviously a couple who've been together for decades, and all they can afford is a single meal. Eventually, a young onlooker wanders over and offers to buy another meal.

'We're just fine, thanks,' says the pensioner. 'After 50 years, we're used to sharing everything.'

Then the young man notices that the little old lady hasn't eaten a bite of her portion. Instead, while her husband wolfs down his half, she sits and occasionally sips the drink.

'Ma'am,' says the young chap. 'Why aren't you eating? Your husband says you share everything. What are you waiting for?'

Over horn-rimmed glasses, she looks back at him. 'The teeth,' she says.

## Marital economics

Little Johnny walks past his parents room one night and sees them making love. Puzzled, he asks his father about it in the morning. 'Why were you doing that to mummy last night?'

His father replies, 'Because mummy wants a baby.'

The next night, Johnny spots mummy giving daddy a blow job and the next morning he asks his father, 'Why was mummy doing that to you last night?'

His father replies, 'Because mummy wants a BMW.'

## Overheard ... at the racecourse

**Carpet:** Rug-like description of 3/1 odds.

**Connections:** People closely involved with the horse, especially the owner and the trainer.

**Ear'ole:** Odds of 6/4.

**Faces:** People with inside information. Nothing to do with Rod Stewart.

**Headquarters:** Newmarket.

**Jolly:** Cheery *nom de plume* of the favourite.

**Layers:** The bookmakers.

**Monkey:** £500 in real money.

**Pony:** £25.

**Rag:** A horse with little chance of winning.

**Steamer:** A heavily backed nag.

**Plum:** £1,000.

**Double carpet:** Odds of 33/1.

**Canadian plus:** Twenty-six bets on five selections.

**Heinz plus:** Fifty-seven bets on six selections.

**Patent:** Seven bets on three selections.

**Trixie:** Four bets on three selections.

**Yankee plus:** Eleven bets on four selections.

## Two countries separated by a common language

A tourist walks into a drug store in Los Angeles, and asks for a packet of condoms. 'Rubbers, eh?' says the chemist, recognizing his customer is English. 'That'll be five dollars – including the tax.'

'Is that necessary?' cries the man. 'Back home, we roll them on.'

## The taxman cometh

A Yuletide meal at an expensive restaurant is disturbed when a woman starts screaming. 'My son's choking! ' she cries. 'He's swallowed the sixpence in the Christmas pudding! Please, anyone – help!'
Without speaking, a man stands up at a nearby table, and walks over nonchalantly. Smiling pleasantly, he grips the boy by the gonads and squeezes: the boy coughs, and out pops the coin.
'Thank you so much!' beams the relieved mother. 'Are you a paramedic?'
'No,' replied the man, 'I work for the Inland Revenue.'

## Builders' arse

One day a construction crew arrives next door to a young family to build another house. The family's six-year-old daughter naturally takes an interest, and begins hanging around the site. Eventually the brickies adopt her as a kind of mascot – chatting to her and giving her errands to run. Then, at the end of the week, they present her with a pay envelope containing a fiver.
Excitedly, the little girl runs home to her mother, who suggests they take it to the bank. Running straight up to the pay-in desk, the little girl thrusts her wages over the counter.
'I earned this building a house,' she beams, proudly. 'For a whole week.'
'Goodness!' smiles the teller. 'And will you be building it next week, too?'
'Yes,' trills the little girl. 'If the fucking bricks ever get delivered.'

## Calling all cars ...

A burglary was recently committed at Manchester City's ground and the entire contents of the trophy room were stolen. Police are looking for a man with a pale blue carpet.

## Know your own strength

Sven Goran Eriksson arrives for his first training session as England manager, and wanders into the changing room – only to spot a massive, steaming turd nestling in the middle of the shower room. Fuming, he returns to his players in the main changing area.
'Who's shit on the floor?' he screams.
'Me, boss,' cries Emil Heskey, 'but I'm not bad in the air.'

# Can I get some privacy?

Little Red Riding Hood is walking through the woods one day, when she spies the wolf crouched down behind a bush. Thinking that it would be a laugh and make a bit of a change to sneak up on him for once, she creeps over and taps the wolf on his shoulder.

'My, mister wolf,' she says with a smirk, 'what big eyes you have. Don't you want to play?'

'Leave me alone!' the wolf cries, and runs off. Riding Hood trails him for a way, and finds him behind an old oak tree.

'My, mister wolf,' she says, 'what big ears you have. Don't you want to play?'

'For God's sake, please leave me alone!' the beast howls, and runs off into the woods. Riding Hood strikes out after him, and discovers him in a patch of old stinging nettles.

'My, mister wolf,' she says, 'what big teeth you have. Don't you want to play?'

'For Christ's sake, leave me alone!' the wolf barks in fury. 'I'm trying to have a shit!'

# The awkward customer

Cursed with a bald head and a wooden leg, a man is surprised to learn that he's been invited to a fancy dress party. Deciding that he might pull it off if he wears a costume to hide his head and leg, he writes to a theatrical outfitters asking them for advice. A few days later, he receives a parcel from the company with a note that says, 'Dear sir. Please find enclosed a pirate's outfit. The spotted handkerchief will cover your bald head, and with your wooden leg you will be just right as a buccaneer.'

Unfortunately, the man finds this deeply insulting, as they have so clearly emphasized his wooden leg, so he fires off a letter of complaint. A week passes before the postman delivers another parcel with a note that reads, 'Dear sir, sorry about our previous suggestion – please find enclosed a monk's habit. The long robe will cover your wooden leg and with your bald head you will really look the part.'

This infuriates the man again, because they have simply switched from emphasizing his wooden leg to his balding head, so he writes the company another letter of complaint. The next day he receives a tiny parcel and a hastily scrawled note, which reads:

'Dear sir, please find enclosed a tin of treacle. Pour it over your head, stick your wooden leg up your arse and go as a toffee apple, you grumpy twat.'

## Justice, South African style

Three men in a prison in South Africa; two white, one black. The first white guy says, 'I'm in for six years for robbery. The judge said I was lucky. If it had been armed robbery, I would have got ten.'

The second white man says, 'I'm in for 15 years for manslaughter. The judge said I was lucky. If it had been first degree murder, I would have got more than 20.'

The black man says, 'I got 20 years for riding without my bicycle lights on. The judge says I was lucky. If it had been dark at the time, he would have given me life.'

## Overheard ... in South Africa

**Gentoo:** A whore. In the 19th century, a ship called the Gentoo landed in South Africa. Much to the resident Afrikaners' delight it was full of prostitutes.

**Soutpeil:** An English South African who can't decide what country he is from. Soutpeil translates as 'salt penis', referring to the fact that the man has one foot in each country, leaving his knob dangling in the ocean.

**Koffie-moffie:** Disparaging term for an airline steward.

**Witblits:** A very strong, clear spirit, brewed at home and made from grapes which have already been pressed for wine-making.

**A chalkdown:** What happens when teachers go on strike.

**The ore:** Nothing to do with gold mines, this is the nickname for the Johannesburg police force.

**Opstoker:** A troublemaker.

**Esel:** Originally a type of donkey, but now applied to anyone considered to be of limited intelligence. As in 'That Koffie-moffie spilt beer all over me, the fucking esel.'

**Goosie:** How Afrikaners refer to their girlfriends when insulting them. A goosie is a partner who is willing to dole out sexual favours.

**The hairybacks:** How the black population often refer to the notoriously hirsute Afrikaners.

## Holiday dilemma

The Good Lord is up in Heaven, moaning about the pressures and stresses of omnipotence and being Number One. He decides it's time to go on holiday. He summons all his superbeing mates and they pop round with a few suggestions. 'What about Mars?' says one.

'Nah,' replies God. 'I went there 15,000 years ago, and it was awful – no atmosphere and too dusty.'

'Pluto?' suggests another.

'No way,' God pipes up. 'I went there 10,000 years ago. Freezing. Awful place.'

'Well,' says another of God's protegés. 'How about Mercury?'

God turns the suggestion down. 'Been there. Nearly burnt my nuts off – never again.'

'Okay,' says another of God's favourite cronies. 'How about Earth?'

'Woah!' God exclaims. 'Not a chance! I went there about 2,000 years ago, knocked up some bird and they're still bloody talking about it!'

## The numbers game

A man is strolling past a lunatic asylum when he hears a loud chanting. 'Thirteen! Thirteen! Thirteen!' goes the noise from within the mental hospital's wards.

The man's curiosity gets the better of him and he searches for a hole in the security fence. It's not long before he finds a small crack, so he leans forward and peers in. Instantly, someone jabs him in the eye.

As he reels back in agony, the chanting continues:

'Fourteen! Fourteen! Fourteen!'

## The usual, sire?

Good King Wenceslas phones up his local Italian takeaway.

'I'll have a pepperoni pizza, please,' requests the monarch.

'Certainly, your Majesty' says the Manager, 'Would you like your usual?'

'Yes please,' replies the King. 'Deep pan, crisp and even.'

# Load of balls

While holidaying in southern Spain a man visits a local restaurant – where he sees a diner happily wolfing down two large pink objects. 'I'll have those, please,' he tells the waiter.

'I'm sorry, Senor,' comes the reply, 'but they are cojones – the testicles of the bull killed in the local bullfight. We won't have any more until after the next fight.'

Disappointed, the man returns after the next fight. The waiter remembers him and brings out a plate of two steaming balls. 'Just a minute,' says the man. 'These are tiny. The ones the man had were four times as big.'

The waiter shrugs. 'Senor – sometimes the bull, he win.'

# Good dog!

There were three rottweilers in the waiting room at the vet's surgery, and after a while they got talking.

'I was out walking with my master,' says the first one, 'when a thug attacked him, so I chased the guy, caught him by the throat and savaged him to death. That's why I'm here to be put down.'

'I was in the house,' began the second dog, 'when a burglar broke in and tried to nick the TV. So I pinned him to the floor, bit his arm off, and now I'm here to be put down.'

The third rottweiler then started his story. 'I was patrolling the house one evening, and I wandered into the bathroom to see my master's wife naked, bending over the tub, so I leapt up and gave her a good seeing-to from behind.'

'What, and you're being put down for that?'

Oh, no. I'm just here to get my claws clipped.'

# Short tempered

The supervisor of a local firm is somewhat startled when his secretary bursts into his office and demands to file a complaint of sexual harassment against a man who works in the same department.

'What on earth did he do?' asks the concerned boss.

'It's not what he did, it's what he said!' she shrieks. 'He said that my hair smelt nice!'

'And what's so wrong with telling you that?' asks the supervisor, confused.

'He's a midget,' huffs the woman.

## Going bats

Two bats are out searching for a midnight feed. After a while they reunite at the belfry. Boris is still starving, not having found a thing to eat. But Brian comes in licking his lips, fresh blood oozing from his mouth and fangs.
'Wow', exclaims Boris. 'I couldn't even find a mouse to eat. Where on earth did you get all that from?'
'Come on, I'll show you', replies Brian, and off they venture into the night. After a few moments, Brian slows to a hover and whispers, 'Right. See that tree?'
'Uh-huh', murmurs Boris.
'I didn't', says Brian.

## Loaded for bear

An extremely wealthy 80-year-old man arrived for his annual check-up and smiled when the doctor enquired about his health.
'Never better', he announced proudly. 'I've taken an 18-year-old bride, and she's pregnant. What do you think of that?'
The doctor considered this for a moment, then said, 'I once knew a guy who was an avid hunter. One day he slept late and in the subsequent rush, he

dashed out with his umbrella instead of his rifle.'

'Go on, doc,' says the old-timer.

'Deep in the woods, he faced a huge, angry bear, raised his umbrella, pointed it at the animal and squeezed the handle. And do you know what happened?' Dumbfounded, the old codger shook his head.

'The bear fell dead in front of him.'

'That's impossible,' exclaimed the old man. 'Someone else must have been doing the shooting.'

Sighing, the doctor gave his patient a friendly pat on the back.

'That's what I'm getting at.'

# I dream of genie

Bill is sitting in a pub and pulls out a tiny piano and a little guy about a foot tall. The little guy sits down and starts playing the piano quite beautifully. The fellow on the next bar stool, Joe, says, 'That's amazing. Where did you get him?'

Bill says, 'Well, I got this magic lamp with a genie inside. He granted me one wish.'

'That's great, could I use it?'

Bill agrees, and hands him the lamp. Joe rubs it and out pops the genie who offers him anything he wants. He says, 'I want a million bucks.'

Suddenly the room is entirely filled with quacking ducks. Joe exclaims, 'Hey! I asked for a million BUCKS! Not DUCKS!'

Bill explains, 'Yes, he's a bit deaf, isn't he? You don't think I asked for a 12-inch pianist?'

# Right-winger

After a heavy night in his local pub, a worse-for-wear lout rises to his feet, determined to start up a fight.

'Right,' he hollers, 'everybody on the left side of the pub is a bastard!'

The drinkers look across at him briefly, then resume their drinking.

'No takers, eh?' shouts the piss-head. 'Right then – everyone on the right side is a poofter!'

Suddenly, an old man on the left-hand side of the pub stands up. 'You want some, then?' screams the lout.

'Not really,' replies the man, sheepishly. 'It's just that I appear to be sitting on the wrong side of the pub.'

## Farmer in the dock

A well-known farmer is caught in a mindless act of bestiality with an ox on his farm, and – after much public humiliation and ridicule from the police – looks up both the village lawyers. He finds himself faced with two choices. The first lawyer has a brilliant reputation of finding a sympathetic jury, but has a history of making ludicrous statements and summing up in a disastrous fashion. The second is a fantastic debater and a real case-winner, but is always plagued by juries that want to lynch him. The farmer eventually settles on the first lawyer.

A week later, sitting in court, his lawyer stands, adjusts his tie and turns to the jury. 'My client,' he says confidently, 'approached the ox from behind, took it by surprise, grabbed it hard by its flanks, and went at it hell for leather. When he had finished, he casually walked round to the front of the beast, who proceeded to lick his penis clean.'

The farmer stares at his lawyer in disbelief, cursing himself for hiring such an obvious simpleton, when suddenly the jury nod enthusiastically and the foreman whispers, 'Mmm, yes – a good ox will do that.'

## Mistaken identity

Feeling rather daring, a grey-haired old woman goes to a tattoo parlour. 'I want a picture of Frank Bruno on my left inner thigh and a picture of Mike Tyson on my right inner thigh,' she says to the tattooist.

When he's finished, she looks at her new tattoos. Disgusted, she says, 'These are rubbish! I want to see the manager.'

The manager comes out, 'What seems to be the problem, madam?' he asks. 'I wanted a tattoo of Frank Bruno and Mike Tyson and they don't look like either of them!'

The manager steps back to take a look. 'You're right, they don't. But the one in the middle is definitely Don King.'

## Are you local?

Hopelessly lost, a businessman approaches a local in a village. 'Excuse me,' he says, 'but what's the quickest way to York?' The local scratches his head. 'Are you walking or driving?' he asks. 'I'm driving,' comes the reply. 'Hmm,' mulls the local. 'I'd say that's definitely the quickest way.'

## Sticky wicket

The Lone Ranger and his faithful red Indian chum, Tonto, are riding down
a hillside in the Wild West, when Tonto suddenly stops, gets off his horse
and puts his head to the ground.
'Buffalo come,' Tonto said.
'Amazing! How do you know?' asks the Lone Ranger.
'Ear stuck to ground,' replies Tonto.

## Overheard ... cowboys

**Airin' the paunch:** Getting rid of a few excess calories by vomiting.

**Axle grease:** Butter for your sarnie.

**Bar dog:** Moustachioed bartender.

**Bean master:** The cook, also known as the dough wrangler.

**Brown gargle:** Good coffee.

**Belly wash:** Bad coffee.

**Black-eyed Susan:** A six-gun.

**Bob wire:** Cowboy's attempt at saying barbed wire.

**Can openers:** Spurs.

**Hair case:** Hat.

**Neck oil:** Whiskey.

**Necktie party:** Not a posh do, but a public hanging.

**Prairie oyster:** A fried calf's testicle.

**Sand:** Courage, as in grit.

**Top waddy:** Highly-skilled, Wayne-esque cowboy.

**Whistleberries:** Beans.

## Sweet chastity

A brave knight has to go off to fight in the Crusades and leaves his sexy wife
at home. As he can't trust his wife to be left on her own, he fits her with a
very special chastity belt made out of razor blades. On his victorious return,
he lines up all his male staff, and makes them drop their trousers. He is
greeted by a whole line of shredded todgers, apart from one. He goes up to
that man and said, 'I trusted you and, unlike all the others, you have not
betrayed my trust. In return I shall give you half my land.'
To which the man replies, 'Ugg ou gery muk.'

# What do you expect from a horse?

Roy Rogers is riding through the Wild West on his trusty horse, Trigger, when he happens upon Apache Indians. Not best pleased at having trespassers in their territory, the Indians capture Roy and bury him up to his chin in the sand. Before leaving him to die in the scorching heat, the Indians grant him one last wish. 'Could I say a parting farewell to my trusty steed?' comes the request. The Indians seem to understand, and agree, so Roy beckons Trigger to come closer then whispers in his ear. The horse bolts off at once in the direction of the nearest town.

Half an hour later, the horse returns bearing a scantily clad, gorgeous prostitute. The prostitute jumps down off the horse and gently removes the small, frilly knickers she's wearing. Sitting astride Roy Rogers' face, she proceeds to give him firsts, seconds and thirds of her fanny, almost suffocating him in the process.

Well, the Indians think this is magic and decide that he deserves another wish. So Roy beckons his horse again and whispers in his ear.

'I said fetch a posse, you stupid git!'

# Smells funny

After years of flirting, a man and woman in an old people's home agree to make love – and one day, when the residents go on a day trip, they both stay behind. Impatient for his first action in decades, the man quickly goes to the woman's room and asks her if there's anything she prefers. She replies she loves it when men perform cunnilingus on her – and grinning widely, the man goes down.

After a few seconds, however, he reappears. 'I'm sorry,' he says, 'but I'm afraid the smell is just too bad.'

'Hmmm,' she replies, thinking for a moment. 'It must be the arthritis.'

He looks at her confused. 'Surely you can't get arthritis down there,' he cries, 'And even if you could, it wouldn't cause that smell.'

'No, the arthritis is in my shoulder,' she bleats. 'I can't wipe my arse.'

# Surprise package

At the end of the primary school term, a kindergarten teacher is receiving gifts from her departing pupils. First up is the local florist's son, whose gift is

a well-wrapped cone. 'I bet I know what it is,' she says, after shaking it and inhaling deeply. 'Have you got me flowers?'

'That's right!' cries the boy. 'But how did you know?'

'Just a wild guess,' she said, grinning.

The next pupil was the daughter of the local sweetshop owner. Again, the teacher held her box over her head, shook it, and heard the soft rattle.

'Thank you,' she says, 'I love chocolates!'

'That's right! But how did you know?' asked the girl.

'Just a lucky guess,' laughs the teacher.

Finally, the son of the local off-licence owner shyly approaches. Again, the teacher holds his box above her head and shakes it side to side – only to find it leaking.

'Mmmm,' she says, tasting a drop of the leakage with her finger. 'Is it wine?'

Open-mouthed, the youngster shakes his head – and the teacher repeats the process. 'Oh. Is it a nice vintage champagne, perhaps?' she asks.

Again, the boy shakes his head excitedly.

'OK,' admits the teacher, 'I give up. What is it?'

The boy laughs in delight. 'A puppy!'

## The Mexican bandit

Two young travellers are braving their way across Mexico behind the wheel of an old van, when they come across a group of bandits standing behind a roadblock. The head honcho walks around to the door, sticks a gun into their faces and says, 'Start masturbating, gringos!'

Shocked, but fearing for their lives, the pair duly oblige – and, despite the stress, manage to perform.

As soon as they finish, the bandit chief leans in and demands: 'Again!' They manage a repeat performance, but are then told to continue until, tired and sore, the pair are physically incapable of another erection.

'Good work,' smiles the toothless Mexican as a dark figure emerges from the trees. 'Now drive my sister to the nearest town.'

## Overheard ... at a London market

**The joint:** The pitch, where the trader builds his stall each day.

**A schnorrer:** 'How much is this? How much is that?' asks the schnorrer, before wandering off empty-handed half an hour later because everything is too expensive.

**Sore one:** A bad day – everybody with a stall has them.

**Cavalry:** A customer who spends freely on a 'sore one' (qv), thus 'rescuing' the trader.

**A dog:** Not man's best friend, but a rotter who steals a traders' pitch.

**Grass:** Asparagus.

**Jack and Jill:** It's where you find the money, because it's the till.

**On the penny:** Cheap.

**Richard:** Confusingly, a young lady. From Richard the Third – bird.

**Dlo:** Imaginatively pronounced 'dee-lo', it's old stock – 'old' spelt backwards.

**Jekyll:** Another rhymer, it means 'snide', which in turn also means bad stock. Don't buy it!

## One for Beatles fans

What would it take to reunite the Beatles?
Three bullets.

## Desert island dicks

A man who has been shipwrecked on a desert island for several years is beginning to feel the effects of being starved of sex for so long. However, the only living creatures on the island are a pig and a dog. One day, the man decides he's had enough and thinks to himself that it has to be the pig. But when he approaches the sow for his moment of passion, the dog bites the man's backside. This continues for several days, and the man is beginning to get very frustrated.

But one morning, the man's luck changes: out to sea, he notices a beautiful young woman on the point of drowning. He swims over, drags her out on to the beach and proceeds to give her the kiss of life. The woman comes to and is very grateful.

'Thank you so much,' she says. 'I will do anything for you, and I mean absolutely anything.'

The man can't believe his luck and quickly replies, 'You wouldn't mind taking that bloody dog for a walk, would you?'

## The mumbling midget

One morning, a stud farm owner receives a visit from a midget wanting to buy a horse. It soon becomes obvious that the dwarf has a bad speech impediment. 'Can I view a female horth?' he asks.

Dutifully, the owner leads one out, and shows the midget the hoofs and legs. 'That'th a thtrong looking beatht, for thure,' says the gnomic breeder, nodding his head. 'Can I thee her mouf?'

Confused as to how the tiny man will ride the animal, the farmer still picks up the midget by his braces and shows him the horse's mouth.

'Nith, healthy-looking horth,' agrees the midget. 'Now move me awownd to her eerth ...'

Now getting annoyed, the owner lifts up the midget one more time to look at the ears.

'Finally,' says the Lilliputian, 'can I see her twat?'

With that, the owner picks up the midget and shoves his head into the horse's vagina. He pulls him out after a minute, and the tiny man stumbles around, dazed.

'Perhapth I thould rephrathe that,' says the midget, shaking his head. 'Can I thee her wun awownd?'

## Never satisfied

Two rabbits, who have spent their whole lives in a laboratory, are set free one night by an animal activist. They run off into the countryside and come across a field of carrots. Instinct takes over: they get stuck in and start to eat all the carrots they can, until they fall asleep.

The following night, they go into a field of cabbages. Again, they eat all they can and fall asleep. The night after that, they find a field full of lettuce, which, as before, they proceed to chomp through until they fall asleep.

The next night they find themselves in a field full of lady rabbits, all of whom are willing partners. They do what comes naturally and embark upon an all-night shagging session. In the morning, the older rabbit decides he wants to return to the lab.

'What the hell for?' asks his pal. 'We've had carrots, cabbages, lettuce and, best of all, those ladies last night. What's your problem?'

'Life is sweet, I agree,' says the older chap. 'But the thing is, I'm dying for a fag!'

## Moo!

Two cows in a field. One says to the other,
'What do you make of this mad cow disease?'
The other one says, 'Doesn't affect me, mate.'
'Oh, yeah? Why's that?'
'I'm a helicopter.'

# Earning her money

Knowing that he'll be back late from work, Joe asks his workmate Barry to pop by his house to let his wife know what time he'll be home. Barry agrees and sets off. Joe's wife opens the door and invites Barry in, as she's just finishing her ironing. Barry passes on his news and notices that Joe's wife is ironing her underwear.

'I tell you what,' says Barry. 'I know you're a bit hard up at the moment, so if you dance around for me in that underwear, I'll give you £40.'

Needing the money, she reluctantly agrees. After the dance, Barry continues, 'Now I'll make it £100 if you do that naked.' A little sheepishly, she strips off her undies and repeats the dance.

'Now,' says an excited Barry, 'I'll make it £200 if you let me give you one.' Feeling ashamed but desperate for the money, she again agrees. When Barry finishes, he thanks her, pays her the money and leaves. Thirty minutes later, Joe returns from work to find his wife watching the telly.

'All right, love? Did Barry tell you I'd be late?' Still embarrassed, she nods. 'Oh, and love,' Joe goes on, 'did he give you my wages?'

# The fearless firemen

During a particularly dry summer, a chemical plant bursts into flames, and the alarm goes out to all available fire departments. Twenty engines duly arrive, and spend the next three hours battling the inferno. Eventually, with little sign of the fire being put out, the company director runs over and says:

'All of our industrial secrets are still in there. I'll offer £50,000 to any team that can salvage them.'

With renewed vigour, the firemen try to quench the flames, but to no avail. Suddenly, a dilapidated old engine with a volunteer crew of geriatrics comes screaming down the street, straight into the middle of the inferno. The other firefighters can only watch in awe as the old fellas hop out and bring the flames under control in ten minutes.

As he writes out the cheque, the company director says to the chief fireman: 'You old boys have done a great job. But tell me, what will you do with the money?'

The smoke-addled elderly gent peers at him, coughs, and says:

'Well, the first thing is to get some fucking brakes for that truck.'

## Be gentle with me

A bloke walks into the doctor's surgery looking very sheepish. The doctor asks him what the problem is and he explains that it's a rather delicate matter to do with his back passage, which he finds a bit difficult to talk about.

The doctor says, 'Look, I've been in this profession for 26 years and there isn't much I haven't seen. I understand you're embarrassed about it, but it would save us both a lot of time if you just told me.'

'I think I'd find it a lot easier if I just showed you,' the man replied. The doctor agrees, so the man drops his trousers and bends over. The sight of the guy's arsehole renders the doctor speechless; it has been torn to the size of a football and is badly bruised.

'Jesus Christ!' said the doctor, 'What the hell happened to you?'

'Well,' the bloke says, 'I was on Safari in Kenya and I got raped by a bull elephant.'

The doctor considers this for a second and says, 'Well, with my rather limited knowledge of veterinary science, I thought elephants' penises were very long and very thin.'

'That's right, doctor,' the guy agrees, 'but he fingered me first.'

## They grow up so fast

Desperate for a Sunday afternoon quickie, Bill and Marla decide that the only way to distract their ten-year-old son long enough is send him out onto the balcony of their flat to report on all the neighbourhood activities.

The boy began his commentary as his parents put their plan into operation.

'There's a car being towed from the parking lot,' he says, after few minutes. 'And now an ambulance is driving past.'

There's a moment's quiet, before the amorous couple hear his narration again: 'Looks like the Andersons have company,' he calls out. 'Matt from no.8 is riding a new bike ... and the Coopers are having sex.'

Mum and Dad shoot up in bed. 'How do you know that?' asks Bill, startled. 'Their kid is standing out on the balcony, too,' his son replied.

## Bringing them round

Two young guys are picked up by the cops for smoking dope and appear in court before the judge. The judge tells them, 'You seem like nice young men, and I'd like to give you a second chance rather than jail time. I want you to go out this weekend and show others the evils of drug use and get them to give up drugs forever. I'll see you back in court on Monday.'

When the two guys return to court, the judge asks the first one, 'So, how did you do over the weekend?'

'Well, your Honour, I managed to persuade 17 people to give up drugs forever.'

'Seventeen people? That's wonderful. What did you tell them?'

'I used a diagram, Your Honour. I drew two circles like this – O o – and explained to them that the big circle is your brain before drugs and that the small circle is your brain after drugs.'

'That's admirable,' said the judge, turning to the second guy. 'And you, how did you do?'

'Well, Your Honour, I managed to persuade 156 people to give up drugs forever.'

'156 people! That's amazing! How did you manage to do that!'

'Well, I used the same diagram, only I pointed to the small circle first and said this is your arsehole before prison ...'

# The perils of gambling

An old man and his grandson went into a betting shop, and the boy asked his grandfather if he could put a bet on. The old man asked his young grandson if he could touch his arse with his dick.

'No,' replied the boy.

'Well then, you're not old enough,' remarked his grandfather.

So the boy went next door to the paper shop to buy a scratch card, which he immediately scratched, to find he had won £50,000. He ran back to his grandpa, who suggested that they split it 50:50.

The boy said, 'Grandfather, can you touch your arse with your dick?'

'Yes, of course. I'm a grown man,' he replied.

'Well then, go fuck yourself.'

# It's that old playground favourite

How do you confuse a dickhead?

Forty-two.

## In the bakers

A Glaswegian walks into a bakers, and looks at the array of cakes on offer.
'Scuse me,' he barks at the assistant, in his thick Scottish brogue. 'But is that a macaroon, or a meringue?'
'No, you're right,' says the woman behind the counter. 'It is a macaroon.'

## The city of love

A young Australian is enjoying his first night in Rome. He's drinking cappuccino at a pavement cafe when a pretty girl sat herself beside him.
'Hello,' he says, 'do you understand English?'
'Only a little,' she replies.
'How much?' he asks.
'Fifty dollars,' she replies.

## Sex education

Young Judith runs out to the backyard, where her father is chopping wood.
She looks up at the hard-working parent, smiles, and asks: 'Daddy, what is 'sex'?'
Laying down his axe, the old-timer sits beside his daughter and starts to explain about the birds and the bees. Then he tells her about conception, sperm and eggs. Next he thinks, 'What the hell – I might as well explain the whole works,' and goes into great detail about puberty, menstruation, erections and wet dreams. Judith's eyes bulge as her old man continues his lesson, moving on to masturbation, oral, anal and group sex, pornography, bestiality, dildos and homosexuality.
Realizing he has probably gone too far, the father pauses and asks,
'So, Judith, why do you want to know about sex?'
'Well,' says the fresh-faced youngster. 'Mummy said to tell you that lunch will be ready in a couple of secs.'

## Slip of the tongue

A guy is talking to his friend and says, 'Man, I made the most embarrassing mistake yesterday. I went to the airport and the woman behind the counter had these beautiful big breasts, and I asked her for two pickets to Tittsburgh!'
'Yeah, I know what you mean,' his friend replied. 'Just this morning I meant to ask my wife to pass the salt and I said 'BITCH, YOU RUINED MY LIFE!'

# For you, the war is over

At the start of World War One, a father approaches his son to explain he has
to go to fight for his country. Nodding, his son asks that on his return could
he bring back a souvenir from the battlefields – perhaps a German helmet.
'You know,' says the boy, 'One with a spike on top.'

And so, weeks later the man is out on the mud-soaked fields of Flanders,
when he spies a German helmet lying in the mud. Bending down to pick it up,
he finds it stuck fast; as he grasps the spike for a better grip, he realizes there
is a German soldier still attached underneath.

'If you pull me out of ze dirt, you can tek me prisoner,' says the soldier,
through the grime.

'If I pull you out,' says the Brit, 'can I have your helmet for my son?'

'Ja – be my guest!' comes the German's cheerful reply.

And so, with great effort, he begins to pull the soldier from the ground. But,
after half an hour, he's still only managed to get him up to his waist.

'I'm bloody knackered,' he says, catching his breath.

'Vud it help,' replies the German soldier, 'Iff I took my feet out of ze stirrups?'

## Open question

A couple of newlyweds are strolling along the beach one morning on honeymoon in Australia. Suddenly the husband spots a fat woman, stark naked, sitting legs akimbo, gorging herself on a fresh watermelon. Excited, he imagines his wife in the same position, and asks her if she would like to feel the sea breeze wafting between her legs? The wife looks at him in disgust.

The next day, they take the same walk, and sure enough the naked woman is there again slobbering over a slice of watermelon. Unperturbed by his wife's earlier refusal, the husband asks again if his bride would like to adopt the large woman's stance and feel the cool air circulate against her fanny? Again, she declines.

This happens everyday for two weeks, until the very last day, when yet again they spot the naked, fat woman.

'Don't you want to know how it feels to have your privates cooled by the salty air?' the husband enquires. And again his missus gets the hump.

'Well, if you're not prepared to try it, why don't you ask her how it feels and see if she can persuade you?' Reluctantly his wife agrees and walks over to the open-legged bloater.

'Er, excuse me, but my husband and I were wondering how it must feel to have the sea breeze wafting over your vagina?' she asked nervously.

'Ah, strewth, I don't know,' says the woman. 'But it sure keeps the flies off my watermelon.'

## Fleas take a break

Two fleas are planning a holiday at the other end of the house. One flea turns to the other and says: 'Should we hop or take the cat?'

## Good reception

A woman rushes into the foyer of a large hotel and sprints up to the reception desk. Seeing that the only member of staff is talking on the phone, she hammers on the bell for service.

The receptionist slowly puts down the phone. 'Yes?' he says, wearily.

'Excuse me,' says the woman, 'But I'm in a frightful hurry. Could you check me out, please?'

The clerk stares at her for a second and looks her up and down.

'Not bad,' he smiles. 'Not bad at all.'

# Lucky motorist

On holiday in Ireland, an American is happily driving through Donegal in the Cadillac he has shipped over from home. But on the third day, his car breaks down, leaving him stranded in the country. He opens the hood but just stands there, staring, not knowing how to fix it.

Then from nowhere he hears a voice saying: 'Check the battery connections.' He turns around but there is no one there. He checks the battery connections and finds them loose, so tightens them up; the car starts and he drives off.

A couple of yards down the road he spots a nice pub and goes in for lunch. He ends up chatting to the barman and tells him of the incident.

'Ah, you must have been at O'Conner's farm,' says the barman.

'I was near a farm – but how do you know it was O'Conner's?' asks the Yank.

'Was there a little bridge?'

'Yes, there was' the man replies.

'And to your left was there a grey mare and a black stallion in the bottom field?' the barman probes.

'Gee, there was,' the holidaymaker retorts.

'Ahh, you're a lucky man,' laughs the publican. 'The grey mare knows nothing about engines.'

# Drunk driving (iii)

While walking his beat, a policeman is bemused to find a young man, clearly drunk, staggering about with a key in his hand.

'They've stolen my car,' the drunk shouts. 'It was right here earlier on the end of this key.'

'More importantly, sir,' says the policeman. 'Do you know your penis is hanging out?'

'Oh my God,' wails the drunk. 'They've got my girlfriend as well.'

# Getting the hump

Quasimodo asks Esmerelda one day if he really is the ugliest man alive. Esmerelda says, 'Go upstairs and ask the magic mirror who is the ugliest man alive and the magic mirror will tell you.'

Five minutes later, Quasimodo comes back and sits down.

After a while, Esmerelda says, 'Well?'

To which Quasimodo says, 'Who's Iain Dowie?'

## Wrong number

A rich man is away on a business trip and phones home. The maid answers and he asks if he can speak to his wife.

'She's upstairs having sex with her lover,' the undiplomatic home-help replies.

'Right,' says the man, 'go upstairs. Take out my shotgun and shoot them both.'

The maid leaves, and the man hears two loud shots, then the maid returns.

'What shall I do with the bodies?' she asks.

'Take them out the back,' the man says. 'And dump them in the swimming pool.'

'What swimming pool?' the maid asks.

'That is 849 9698, isn't it?' asks the man.

## Ye Gods!

Thor, the Viking God of Thunder, and Odin, the King Of The Gods, are enjoying a flagon of mead in Valhalla, the Norse heaven. Suddenly, Thor turns to Odin.

'You know, my Lord,' he says, thoughtfully thumbing his mystical hammer.

'Being a god is brilliant, but it's been millennia since I had any sex.'

Odin nodded and pondered for a while. Raising his mighty head, he took pity on his subordinate.

'Go to Earth, Thor,' he replied. 'Find thyself there what they call a "lady of the night". Treat her to your manly pleasures.'

Bowing gracefully, Thor retired and followed Odin's advice, before returning the next night.

'My Lord,' he said, grinning from ear to ear, 'You were right – it was wonderful. We had passionate sex 37 times!'

'Thirty-seven times?' exclaimed Odin. 'That poor woman! Mere mortals cannot endure such treatment. You must go and apologize this instant!'

Humbled, Thor went back down to earth and found the prostitute.

'I'm sorry about last night,' he apologized. 'But you see, I'm Thor.'

'You're Thor?' shouted the girl, 'What about me? I can't even pith.'

## Cowboy bluffs it out

A cowboy rode into town and stopped at a saloon. Unfortunately, the locals had a habit of picking on strangers, and when he finished his drink, he found his horse had been stolen. He went back into the bar, flipped his gun in the air, caught it above his head without looking and fired a shot into the ceiling.

'Which one of you sidewinders stole my horse?' he bellowed, making the glasses on the bar shake.

No one answered. The cowboy squinted around the room then, without looking, shot the tops off three bottles of whisky on the bar.

'All right,' he snarled at the room in general. 'I'm gonna have another beer, and if my horse ain't back outside by the time I finish, I'm gonna have to do what I done in Texas.'

The locals shifted uneasily in their seats as the cowboy swivelled around suddenly. 'And let me tell you – I really don't want to do what I done in Texas.'

Chairs creaked restlessly, and the cowboy sat at the bar again, and quickly downed another beer. The locals watched as he got up, paid the bill and walked outside – to find his horse back where he'd left it. As the cowboy saddled-up and started to ride out of town, the bartender wandered out of the bar. Unable to contain his curiosity, he approached the lone wanderer.

'Say partner, before you go – what happened in Texas?'

The cowboy turned back, sadly. 'I had to walk home.'

## One thing at a time

Old Mrs Harris goes to the doctor with an embarrassing problem.

'I pass wind all the time,' she says. 'It doesn't smell, and it's completely silent, but it's very uncomfortable. In fact, I've done it 20 times since coming in.'

The quack thinks for a minute then gives her a prescription.

'Try taking these pills for a week and come back and see me then,' he tells her.

The next week, an even more embarrassed Mrs Harris marches in.

'Doctor, I don't know what was in the pills, but my problem is worse! My wind is as bad as ever, but now it stinks too!'

'Calm down,' says the doc. 'Now we've sorted out your sinuses, we'll see to your hearing ...'

## Overheard ... at Eton

**A wet bob:** One who volunteers to spend time afloat, oar in hand, rowing upriver.

**Oppidan:** A thicko, who's presence can only be explained by rich parents.

**Pop:** A club of the most popular boys, elected by the previous year's most popular boys.

**Div:** A lesson.

**Half:** A term, three in a year.

**Slack Bob:** A serving, volleying, umpire-berating, tennis-playing pupil.

**Chambers:** A pause between 'divs' to enjoy a bottle of milk.

**Dame:** Also known as Matron, she's the Hattie Jacques-dimensioned boil-lancer and cough medicine dispenser everyone tries to avoid.

**M'tutor:** Not an African city, but your housemaster.

**Tap:** The school pub.

**Tardy book:** Contains the names of all those boys to be punished by caning, lines or public tweaking for various offences.

**In the bill:** When you're up to your neck in trouble.

**Mess:** A group of students with whom you take tea.

**New tit:** Not a third breast, but a new boy.

# Bad news for new father

A man is waiting nervously for news of his new-born baby when a nurse walks in. 'It's bad news,' she says. 'Your baby is badly deformed.'

Naturally the man tells himself that he will love the baby whatever it looks like. The midwife then leads the man out to the incubators. Passing a baby that is no more than a head, the midwife says 'Brace yourself, dear – your baby is a lot worse than this.'

Finally they arrive at the incubator and the father stares open-mouthed at his child. For there, sitting on the blanket, is a pair of eyeballs blinking away. 'I'm sorry,' offers the midwife.

The man, holding back tears, says, 'It's my baby and I'll look after it the best I can.'

He gives the little eyes a tender wave.

'I wouldn't bother doing that,' says the midwife. 'It's blind.'

# The DIY expert

A wife, frustrated by her husband's bone-idleness around the house, especially in the DIY department, sees cause for concern one day when the toilet clogs up. She decides to ask him if he'd mind seeing to it, and is greeted with a gruff, 'Who do I look like? A toilet cleaner?'

The next day the waste disposal unit seizes up. Summoning all her courage, she says, 'Sorry to bother you, dear. The waste disposal's broken – would you try to fix it for me?'

'Who do I look like? Some sort of plumber? Get me a beer and sod off!' is the reply.

To cap it all, the next day the washing machine goes on the blink and, taking her life in her hands, the wife addresses the sofa-bound slob: 'Darling, I know you're busy, but the washing machine's packed up.'

'Oh, and I suppose I look like a bloody washing-machine man?' her old man says.

Finally fed up, she calls out three different repairmen to come and fix her appliances.

That evening, she informs her husband of this. He frowns angrily and asks, 'So how much will it cost?'

'Well, they said I could pay them either by baking a cake or having sex,' she says.

'What type of cakes did you bake?' he growls.

'Who do I look like? Delia Smith?'

## Back to Priest School

Father Patrick was talking to his replacement in a small village church.
'Father Michael,' he says, 'you'll be looking after my flock from now on.'
'But where do I start?' the young priest replies. 'You've been hearing
confessions for over 50 years, I'll be lost.'

'Don't worry,' says Father Patrick, 'I've written a list of sins and absolutions
on the wall in the confessional box. Look up the sin and it will tell you next
to it what to say. After a while you'll get to know the congregation and
you'll be okay.'

One week later, Father Michael is sitting in the confessional box looking at his
mentor's list when his first visitor arrives. 'Forgive me Father, for I have
sinned,' says a female voice. 'I had to give my husband a gobble last night.'
The priest searches the wall but can't find the correct reply anywhere. In
desperation he pulls open the curtain of the box and stops a choirboy.
'Oi! What did the old priest give for a gobble?'
'A Kit-Kat,' the lad replies.

## The hygenic waiter

On being seated at a restaurant table, a gentleman becomes somewhat
embarrassed when he knocks the spoon off with his elbow. A nearby waiter
calmly picks it up and produces another shiny spoon from his pocket, which
he places on the table.

Suitably impressed, the diner enquires, 'Do all waiters carry spare spoons
on them?'

The waiter replies, 'Indeed, sir, it is in fact company policy, ever since our
efficiency expert determined that 17.8 per cent of our clients knock the
spoon off the table. By carrying a spare spoon on our person, we save on
trips to the kitchen'

After the gentleman has finished his meal and paid the bill, he wanders over
to the same waiter and says to him, 'You will, of course, forgive me, but do
you know you have a piece of string hanging from your fly?'

'Indeed, sir,' the waiter begins, 'Our efficiency expert determined that we were
spending too much time washing our hands after going to the toilet. Thus, by
attaching this piece of string to my penis I avoid touching myself: I go, and
then I return to work. It saves a lot of time.'

'But how do you put it back in your trousers?' asks the curious diner.

'Well sir, I can't speak on behalf of my colleagues, but I just use the spoon.'

## The alligator dash

A very rich man who owns a huge house has a drop-dead gorgeous daughter. He's also interested in alligators and has a sumptuous swimming pool filled with different exotic specimens of the species. One day he decides to throw a party and invites hundreds of people. After everyone has had a few drinks, he announces that anyone who can jump into the pool and make it to the other side alive can have either £1 million or his daughter.

No one is willing to try this, until suddenly there's a splash, and he turns to see a bloke in the pool, swimming as fast as he can to the other side.

Everyone cheers him on, as the alligators try to tear him apart. Amazingly, he makes it to the other side, somewhat ruffled, but completely unharmed. The rich man says, 'I say, that was amazing! So what's it to be: the million or my daughter's hand?'

The hero replies, 'Look mate I don't want your money or your daughter. I just want the bastard who pushed me in!'

## Clever lad

Little 10-year-old Freddie goes for a long weekend with his uncle, a wealthy Hampshire farm owner. One evening, as Uncle John and his wife are entertaining guests with cocktails, they are interrupted by an out-of-breath Freddie who shouts out, 'Uncle John! Come quick! The bull is fucking the cow!' Uncle John, highly embarrassed, takes young Freddie aside, and explains that a certain amount of decorum is required. 'You should have said, "The bull is surprising the cow" – not some filth picked up in the playground,' he says.
A few days later, Freddie comes in again as his aunt and uncle are entertaining. 'Uncle John! The bull is surprising the cows!'
The adults share a knowing grin. Uncle John says, 'Thank you, Freddie, but surely you meant to say the cow, not cows. A bull cannot "surprise" more than one cow at a time, you know ...'
'Yes, he can!' replies his obstinate nephew. 'He's fucking the horse!'

## Whole lotta shaking going on

Alf and Mabel have been married for 60 years, and they live in a home for the old and infirm. One day Alf comes into their room and announces, 'Mabel, I know we've been together for 60 years, and we've been through a lot of hard times together, but I'm afraid I've got some bad news. I'm leaving you.'
'Why?' gasps the shocked old lady.
'I'm going out with Vera next door,' he replies.
'Vera? What does she do for you that I don't?'
'She gives me oral sex,' admits Alf.
'But ... but Alfred, I give you oral sex too,' exclaims Mabel.
'Maybe,' says Alf, 'but you don't have Parkinson's Disease.'

## The power of suggestion

A blonde walks in to her local clinic and asks to see the doctor. When she's admitted, the doctor is a little perturbed to see she's wearing headphones and asks her to remove them.
'I'm afraid I can't or I'll die,' she replies.
'Don't be so ridiculous,' the doctor says, reaching across to snatch them out of her ears. Immediately the woman turns red and falls on the floor.
In the name of science the doctor puts the headphones in his ears.
'Breath in, breath out ...' says a soothing voice.

## Deathbed confession

Becky was on her deathbed with husband, Jake, maintaining a steady vigil by her side. His warm tears splashed upon her face and woke her from her near death slumber. 'My darling Jake,' she whispered.

'Hush my love,' he said.

But she was insistent. 'I need to confess something to you.'

'There's nothing to confess, don't worry yourself.' Jake said tenderly.

'No, no – I must die in peace. I have been unfaithful to you with your father, your brother and your best friend,' she croaked pathetically.

'Hush now, Becky – don't torment yourself, I know all about it,' he said. 'Why do you think I poisoned you?'

## A load of hot air

What's the difference between an airship and 365 blow jobs?

One is a Goodyear, the other is an excellent year.

## The power of photography

While enjoying a drink with his mate one night, Trevor decides to try his luck with an attractive lady sitting by the bar. She lets him join her for a drink and to his surprise asks him to accompany him home. They spend the night hard at it. Finally they finish; Trevor rolls off, pulls out a cigarette and looks for his lighter. He asks his new love if she has a light.

'There might be some matches in the top drawer,' she replies.

Opening the drawer he finds some matches on top of a framed photo of another man. Naturally he begins to worry.

'Is this your husband?' he enquires nervously.

'No, silly,' she replies.

'Your boyfriend then?'

'No,' she replies, snuggling up to him.

'Who is he, then?'

'That's me, before the operation.'

## Lucky dog!

A man and his dog walk into a pub, and turn to the assembled patrons.
'Ladies and gentlemen,' the man announces in a loud voice. 'I bet anyone here
a pint of lager that my dog can talk.'

After much cynical muttering from the tables, the barman finally agrees to
the bet – and is amazed as the hound perches himself on the barstool and
delivers a fascinating diatribe about the situation in Ireland.

'That is truly wondrous,' says the barman, as he pours the man a pint. 'But I
bet you another pint that your pooch can't go and get you a newspaper.'
After a moment's though, the man agrees and slips the dog a crisp fiver.
'And I want the change as well,' he says.

The dog nods and runs out of the pub. But an hour later he still hasn't
returned. Worried, the man goes out to look for him and finds the pup in a
nearby alleyway – shagging a local bitch.

'Oi!' the man yells. 'You've never done this before.'

The dog turns back to the man. 'Well,' he says, 'I've never had the
money before.'

## Bullets cost money, you know

A man goes in to a gun shop for a telescopic rifle sight. The assistant takes one out, points it at the window and says, 'This baby is good, you can see right into my house on the hill over there.'

The man looks through the sights and starts laughing.

'What's so funny?' asks the assistant.

'Well, I can see a naked man chasing a naked woman around your house,' replies the customer.

Snatching the scope back, the assistant looks through the sight – and sure enough, there is his wife being chased by an excited young man. Furious, the assistant says that he will give the man the telescopic sight for free if he can take the man's dick off with one bullet and kill his wife with another.

The man agrees and arranges himself behind the gun and looks through the sight. 'You know what?' he says. 'I think I can do this with one bullet.'

## Sick joke

Two buckets of sick are out for a walk when one of them starts crying.

'What's the matter?' asks the other bucket.

'I was brought up down that alley,' replies the second bucket.

## Declan the crab

Declan the humble crab and Katie the lobster princess were madly and passionately in love. For months they enjoyed an idyllic relationship, until one day Katie scuttled over to Declan in tears.

'We can't see each other anymore,' she sobbed.

'Why?' gasped Declan.

'Daddy says that crabs are too common,' she wailed. 'He says that no daughter of his will marry a creature that walks sideways.'

Declan was shattered, and walked away to drink himself in to oblivion.

That night, the great lobster ball was taking place. The lobster princess refused to join in the merriment. Suddenly the doors opened and Declan the crab strode in. The dancing stopped, and all eyes were on Declan as he made his way over to Katie's father. All could see that he was walking forwards. Step by step he made his way over to the throne and looked the King Lobster in the eye. There was a deadly hush.

Finally, the crab spoke. 'Fuck, I'm pissed.'

## Domestic economics

A newly married couple get their first taste of financial hardship when, one day, the husband comes home, and announces he's redundant. Being a proud man and believing that he should always support his wife, his pride is somewhat hurt. His wife, however, assures him that he still loves him, and that things will get better.

Unfortunately they do not, and when the wife suggests that perhaps she should try to find a job, the husband humbly agrees. But things are not well in jobland, and soon the wife realizes that the only option left to her is to go on the game.

She assures her husband that it is merely a job, and will not affect their relationship. Soon after placing some ads in the local phone boxes, the wife receives her first prospective client. The husband agrees to wait upstairs whilst the client comes round and conducts his business with the wife in the couple's lounge.

The visitor is eager to know how much it costs for 'the full works', and in her nervousness the wife has completely forgotten to discuss prices with her husband. She dashes upstairs and asks him.

'Twenty quid,' he replies. The visitor appears disappointed at this news, claiming he has only got £7. So he asks what he could get for that.

The wife dashes upstairs again. 'He's only got £7, what should we do?' she asks. 'Tell him he can have a hand job for that, but no more,' replies the desperate husband.

The client seems delighted at what the wife has to tell him when she returns, and drops his pants to reveal a huge long cock that is the best-looking specimen the wife has ever seen. Instantly, she runs upstairs to her husband yet again. 'What's the matter now?' he asks.

The wife replies, 'Can you lend me £13?'

## Marriage sucks

How do you stop a woman giving you a blow job?
Marry her.

# Howzat!

A priest goes into a pub to avoid the rain and spies a member of his congregation in there looking miserably in to his pint.

'What's wrong, Brian?' asks the kindly man of God.

'It's my grandfather,' replies Brian. 'He's just died.'

'Well, did you not try to take him to Lourdes and get him cured?'

'We had a whip-round in the pub and I went with him, but we had only been there an hour when he died,' answered Brian.

'Well,' comforts the Priest. 'Sometimes the Lord moves in mysterious ways.'

'I think it was more likely to be the speed of the cricket ball that hit him in the head.'

## Overheard ... at the cricket ground

**Barnacle:** A batsman who stays in but makes runs at an agonizingly slow rate.

**Bunsen:** A widely turning spun ball. (From Cockney rhyming slang – Bunsen burner.)

**Cafeteria bowling:** A series of very bad deliveries, so-called because batsmen can help themselves to free runs.

**Chin muscle (also throat theory):** A bowling attack that relies on bouncers aimed at the throat.

**Crowd catch:** When the spectators applaud a catch which wasn't a real dismissal, but came off the batsman's pads or was put down by the fielder out of sight of the umpire.

**Death row:** The line of slips and gullies.

**Mulligrubber:** A ball which springs higher in to the air than expected after bouncing.

**Plim:** The state of grass the day after rain.

**Sledging:** Ruthless abuse of the batsman by the fielding team.

**Umbrella bowler:** A bowler who can get plenty of deliveries in quickly and be effective if a game is threatened by rain.

# Circus kills

How do you kill an entire circus at once?

Go for the Jugguler.

# Hog heaven

Hoping to start breeding pigs, a farmer goes out and buys some of the finest sows he can find. After several weeks, he notices that none of the pigs are getting pregnant. He calls a vet, who informs him that he should try artificial insemination. The farmer doesn't have the slightest idea what the vet means by this, but undeterred, he asks how he will know when his new purchases have become pregnant. He explains that his pigs will stop standing there and lay down and start rolling around in the mud.

Giving it some thought, the dumb farmer concludes that artificial insemination must require him impregnating his livestock himself – so he loads them into the truck and drives them out into the woods to have sex with them all.

The next morning, the farmer looks out of the window only to see his pigs standing around in the field. Desperately, he takes them out to the woods again and bangs them all twice for good measure before retiring to bed.

The next morning, he wakes up to find the pigs still standing around in the field. 'One more try,' he tells himself, and proceeds to load them up and drive them out to the woods. He spends all day shagging the pigs, and upon returning home, falls straight asleep.

The next morning, he cannot even raise himself to look at the pigs, so he asks his wife to look out and see if they're lying in the mud. 'No', she says. 'They're all in the back of the truck and one of them's honking the horn.'

HONK

HONK!

# Strength in numbers

Hacking his way through dense jungle, an explorer comes across a pygmy standing over a dead elephant.

'Did you kill this?' asked the explorer.

'Yes,' replied the tiny man.

'That's amazing! I've never seen such a thing. What did you use?'

'A club,' shrugged the pygmy.

'It must have been a bloody big club!'

'Indeed it was,' said the pygmy. 'There must have been about 300 of us.'

# A disappointed father

Tommy ran home from school, as he couldn't wait to break his good news.

'Mum, Mum!' he yelled. 'I had sex with my geography teacher today! Dad, Dad! Guess what, I had sex with my geography teacher.'

'I'm proud of you, son,' the father replied, to the mother's disbelief.

'I think now you're old enough to ride your brother's bike.'

Tommy's face dropped in disappointment.

'I can't. My arse hurts.'

# Hard decision

A man goes to his doctor and admits that he has a sexual problem.

'I just can't get it up for my wife any more,' he says.

'Don't worry, Mr Williams,' says the doctor.

'Bring your wife in and I'll see what I can do.'

The couple come in the next day and the doctor asks the wife to remove her clothes. Then he asks her to turn around and jump up and down. He turns to the man.

'You're fine,' he says. 'She didn't give me an erection either.'

# Genuine excuse

Pete rings his boss at work and says, 'Look, I'm really sorry, but I can't come to work today. I'm sick.'

'Sick!' screams his boss. 'Sick! This is the tenth time this month, Pete. Exactly how sick are you?'

'Well,' replies Pete. 'I'm in bed with my 12-year-old sister.'

## A quiet drink spoiled

Three lads are enjoying a quiet night in a pub, when a fourth stumbles in and orders a beer. Spying the group, the drunk stumbles over, points at one of the boys and shouts: 'I've shagged your mum!'

The lads ignored him and returned to their pints. He shouts again: 'Up the arse!' Although irritated, they ignore him again. The drunk stands up again points at the boy and yells: 'Your Mum's sucked my cock!'

The boy looks up wearily. 'You're drunk, Dad. Go home.'

## How the press works

Two boys are playing football in the park when one of them is attacked by a rottweiler. Thinking quickly, his friend rips a plank of wood from a nearby fence, forces it into the dog's collar and twists it, breaking the dog's neck.

All the while, a newspaper reporter who was taking a stroll through the park is watching. He rushes over, introduces himself and takes out his pad and pencil to start his story for the next edition. He writes, 'Manchester City fan saves friend from vicious animal.'

The boy interrupts: 'But I'm not a City fan.'

The reporter starts again: 'Manchester United fan rescues friend from horrific attack.'

The boy interrupts again: 'I'm not a United fan either.'

'Who do you support, then?'

'Liverpool,' replies the boy.

So the reporter starts again: 'Scouse bastard kills family pet.'

## Divine intervention

Father Morrissey wakes up one beautiful morning and decides to bunk off church and play golf instead. He convinces another vicar of his illness and gets him to deliver the sermon, then goes off to the course, praying he won't meet anyone from his congregation. On the first tee, he sees that he has the whole course to himself. Result!

Meanwhile, up in Heaven, Saint Peter turns to God and says: 'You're not going to let a man of the cloth get away with this?' God looks down at Father Morrissey just as he tees off. The ball flies 420 yards, bounces once, then rolls straight into the hole. 'And why on earth did you let him get a hole in one?' The Lord smiles. 'Who is he ever going to tell?' he says.

## Singer mishears crowd

Sir Cliff Richard is performing in Japan on the last leg of a successful world tour. The audience go wild as Cliff asks them if there is anything he can sing especially for them.

'Tits and fanny!' scream the audience.

'I can't sing that,' says Cliff. 'I'm a devout Christian.'

'Tits and fanny!' scream the crowd.

'Oh, come on,' says Cliff.

'Tits and fanny!' scream the crowd.

'Okay, okay,' says Cliff. 'But I don't know how it goes.'

'Tits and fanny ...' sing the crowd in unison. ' ... how we don't talk anymore.'

## Overheard ... in the Navy

**Figmo:** Acronym indicating annoyance at imminent departure. Stands for, 'Fuck it, got my orders.'

**Black gang:** The chaps in the engine room, from days when coal was the navy's fuel of choice.

**A banjo:** Not a five-stringed instrument, but a bit of a ruck.

**Elastoplasts:** Used to be known as sawbones, but not any more. They're the medics.

**Laced:** To indulge in a tot too many from the grog barrel.

**Shit on a shingle:** A popular breakfast dish, involving minced beef atop toast.

**Monty:** Gay. From Montego Bay.

**Keel:** An officer may express dissatisfaction with his men by administering a kick up the keel.

**Pompey:** Portsmouth.

**Guz:** Devonport.

**Samantha Fox:** Not the stacked 1980s pin-up, but the clap, or pox, with which her surname unfortunately rhymes.

**A full house:** Painful combination of gonorrhea and syphilis. At the same time.

**Boards:** The officers, from those things they wear on their shoulders.

**HMS Pepperpot:** HMS Penelope, which has been hit so many times she's riddled with holes.

# Playing through

Some friends were playing a round of golf when they heard shouts in the distance. Looking across, they watched amazed as a buxom lady ran onto the fairway, pulled off some of her clothes and sprinted off up the course. Not two minutes later, two men in white coats appeared and asked which way the woman had gone. They pointed up the course and the two men ran off in that direction.

Bemused, the golfers carried on with their game, but were again disturbed by another man. This time he was staggering over the hill, panting with the effort of carrying two buckets of sand. Between wheezes, the newcomer too asked which way the woman had gone, then tottered away. Increasingly baffled, the golf party ran after the figure. 'What the hell is going on?' they asked.

Gasping, the man explained: 'The lady has escaped from our treatment clinic. She has acute nymphomania, and as soon as she gets all her clothes off, the nearest man is ravished.'

'But why do you need two buckets of sand?' shouted the golfers after him.

'Well, I caught her the last time she escaped,' panted the man. 'This time, I needed a handicap.'

# Three little words

An elderly gentleman shuffles into a newspaper office and asks if he can place a piece in the obituaries section.

'No problem sir', says the young girl behind the desk. 'That'll be a pound per word.'

Nodding slowly, the old man writes 'Doris is dead' on a piece of paper, and forlornly passes it back to the girl.

'Is that all you want to put in it?' asks the girl.

The pensioner looks at her with sad eyes. 'I'm afraid I only have three pounds, my dear', he says, and begins to shuffle out of the door.

The girl, feeling sorry for the old man, says she will go up and speak to the editor. 'Wait – I'll see if we can work something out.'

Moments later, she returns from the office, grinning broadly. 'Good news', she says. 'The editor says you can have another three pounds worth of words.'

Smiling gratefully, the old man takes another piece of paper and thinks for moment. Shakily, he then writes: 'Doris Is Dead. Metro For Sale'.

# Patient takes advice too far

After suffering from severe headaches for years with no relief, Trevor is referred to a headache specialist by his family GP.

'The trouble is', Trevor tells the specialist, 'I get this blinding pain, like a knife across my scalp and ...'

He is interrupted by the doctor, 'And a heavy throbbing right behind the left ear?'

'Yes! Exactly! How did you know?'

'Well, I myself suffered from that same type of headache for many years. It is caused by a tension in the scalp muscles. This is how I cured it: every day I would give my wife oral sex.'

'Is that all it takes?' says Trevor, intrigued.

'Oh no', says the doctor. 'When she came she would squeeze her legs together with all her strength and the pressure would relieve the tension in my head. Try that every day for two weeks and come back and let me know how it goes.'

Two weeks go by and Trevor returns, grinning. 'Doc, I'm a new man! I haven't had a headache since I started this treatment! I can't thank you enough.'

'That's fine', says the doctor. 'I was glad to pass on a personal cure.'

'By the way', says Trevor, standing up to leave. 'You have a lovely home.'

## Divine wisdom
Why did God create Adam before Eve?
To give him a chance to speak.

## The best ferret in the world
A man is having a quiet drink in a pub when a tramp comes up and asks, 'Wanna buy this for £50?' He pulls a ferret from his pocket.
'What the hell would I want to buy that for?' asks the man.
'This ferret will give you the best blow job of your life,' the tramp says.
The guy thinks his leg is being pulled, and tells the tramp to sling his hook. Undeterred, the tramps continues, 'Look, if you don't believe me, take it outside for a free trial.'
The guy takes the ferret out to the back of the pub. Straight away, the animal unzips his trousers and gives him the best blow job of his life. So the guy carries the ferret back into the pub, gives the tramp £50 and takes the animal home.
When his battleaxe of a wife opens the front door, the man proudly holds up the ferret.
'Look what I've bought for £50,' he proclaims.
'What on earth did you buy that for?' she asks angrily.
'This ferret gave me the best blow job of my life!' he exclaims.
'Well,' she says, annoyed. 'What the hell do you want me to do with it?'
The man replies, 'Teach it how to cook – and then fuck off!'

## Bus stop
One day, a well-endowed, attractive young lady is sitting on the bus, when a good-looking fellow gets on and sits opposite her. Attracted to him, she starts smiling flirtatiously. Yet it is to no avail. The man ignores her. Surprised and frustrated, the young woman unbuttons her blouse further to reveal her bounteous cleavage and hitches her skirt up to show her stocking-tops. However, there is still no reaction.
Frustrated beyond belief, she tries a last-ditch attempt to capture his attention: she whips off her knickers, jumps onto his seat and straddles his face. Showing the first signs of emotion, the man smiles and shouts out, 'I may be blind, but I know that smell anywhere – it's Grimsby, my stop!'

## First heard at the Hackney Empire, 1953

A drunk goes to the doctor complaining of tiredness and headaches.
'I feel tired all the time,' he slurs. 'My head hurts, I've got a sore arse and I'm not sleeping. What is it, Doc?'
Frowning, the doctor examines him thoroughly before standing back.
'I can't find anything wrong,' he says. 'It must be the drinking.'
'Fair enough,' replies the lush. 'I'll come back when you sober up.'

## Overheard ... behind bars

**Lamp:** One who scoffs at personal hygiene. From paraffin lamp – tramp.
**Crib/Peter/Home:** They're all your bed.
**White Windsor:** A lowly type, from the prison issue soap – the quality lag buys his own.
**In for touching a dog's arse:** TDA – taking cars and driving them away.
**Screw:** A warder, but that's 'Guv' to you, Sonny Jim.
**Kitting:** Passing bad cheques.
**Joey:** In some jails a grass, in others an illicit smuggled package.
**On the out:** The condition of not being behind bars.
**Civvies:** Filter-tipped smoking products.
**A cell spin:** When the authorities rearrange your furniture, in search of things you shouldn't be in possession of.
**Having a pop:** Leave before you're supposed to.
**In patches:** Wearing the stripes awarded to someone who's had a pop and failed.
**Nitto!:** Careful, everyone. Warders!
**Turtle:** Shy chap who rarely strays from his cell.

## Making a boob

A doctor is examining a girl of admirable proportions. Holding his stethoscope up to her chest, he says, 'Okay, big breaths!'
'Yeth,' said the girl, 'and I'm only thixteen...'

# Three hard rats

Three rats are relaxing in a bar. After a few jugs they start talking about how tough they are. The first rat says, 'When I woke up there was a matchbox of Rat-o-kill outside my hole. I ate the whole lot and didn't feel a thing.'
After a significant pause and a few more glasses, the second rat chips in, 'When I got up this morning, there was an enormous rat trap with a huge piece of prime cheese for bait. I stepped up, caught the bar on my back, ate the cheese and slipped out without even a bruise.'
At this, the third rat gets up and heads for the door.
'Where are you going?' ask the two other rats.
'Aw, I'm bored here. Think I'll go home and shag the cat again.'

# Caught short

Two dwarfs have just won the Lottery, so they go out and hire two prostitutes and two hotel rooms. The first dwarf tries desperately all night to get an erection, but all he can hear from the next room is, 'One, two, three, huh!' This goes on all night.
The next morning, the second dwarf asks, 'So, how did it go?'
The first dwarf replies, 'Shit, I couldn't get an erection. How was your night?'
The second dwarf turns round and replies, 'Even worse, I couldn't even get on the bed.'

# More camels ...

The recruit had just arrived at a Foreign Legion post in the desert, and asked his corporal what the men did for recreation. The corporal smiled wisely and said, 'You'll see.'
The young man was puzzled. 'Well, you've got more than a hundred men on this base and I don't see a single woman.'
'You'll see,' the corporal repeated.
That afternoon, 300 camels were herded in the corral. At a signal, the men went wild: sprinting into the enclosure and screwing the camels. The recruit saw the corporal hurrying past him and grabbed his arm.
'I see what you mean, but I don't understand,' he said. 'There must be over 300 camels and only a hundred of us. Why is everybody rushing? Can't a man take his time?'
'What?' exclaimed the corporal, startled. 'And get stuck with an ugly one?'

## Tall order

A milkman is making his deliveries and finds a note attached to a customer's door saying, 'I need 45 gallons of milk.'

He knocks at the door and a beautiful, dumb blonde answers it.

'Is this a mistake?' the milkman asks.

'No,' she says. 'I was watching a talk-show and it said bathing in milk is a good aphrodisiac.'

'Really?' replies the milkman. 'Do you want that pasteurized?'

'No, up to my tits will be fine,' she says.

## The ungrateful wife

A middle-aged woman reads a magazine article which claims that, as women get older, their fannies grow. Concerned about this (and her husband's reaction), she decides to carry out her own test. She places a mirror on the bathroom floor and stands over it, legs apart. While looking down, her husband happens to walk past.

'Watch out!' he cries and jumps at her, pushing her over.

'What are you doing?' the woman shouts. 'You could have broken my arm!'

'Don't be so ungrateful,' her husband replies. 'If you'd fallen down there, you could have broken your neck.'

## Crafty seadog

In search of adventure, an attractive young lady decides to head to the Far East and stows away on the first available ship. After a month, the ship's captain finds her – and is surprised that after a month at sea she's well fed and cared for. He realizes that she must have befriended someone on board, but is surprised when she confesses that it was his first officer. Apparently every morning he would give her a full English breakfast and a bath, and had said that he would continue to do so until they reached Japan.

'And what did he ask in return?' queried the captain.

'You might say he took advantage,' blushed the beauty.

'Too bloody right he did, ' chuckled the old sea dog. ' You're on the Liverpool to Birkenhead ferry.'

## Million-dollar question

A teenager comes home from school and asks his dad, 'What's the difference between potential and reality?'

His dad says, 'I'll show you. Ask your mum if she'd sleep with Robert Redford for a million dollars. Then ask your sister if she'd sleep with Brad Pitt for a million dollars.'

So the kid goes to ask his mum, 'Would you sleep with Robert Redford for a million dollars?' His mum says, 'Don't tell your father, but yes, I would.'

Then he asks his sister, 'For a million dollars, would you sleep with Brad Pitt?' She says, 'Yes!'

The kid goes back to his dad and says, 'I've got it. Potentially we're sitting on two million bucks – but in reality, we're living with a couple of slags.'

## The bear truth

A baby polar bear is sitting on an iceberg with his mum. Suddenly he asks, 'Mummy, am I really a polar bear?' His mother replies, 'Why of course, dear.' A minute later, he asks again, 'Mummy, am I really a polar bear?'

His mum says, 'I'm a polar bear, your daddy is a polar bear, you are a polar bear. Now carry on eating your seal!'

A minute later, the baby asks the question again. Annoyed, the mother shouts, 'Yes! Why do you keep asking?'

To which the baby shrieks, 'Because I'm fucking freezing!'

## It always comes in higher ...

The police have just arrested Fred West. They take him down to the cells and start to interrogate him. They say, 'Right then, you bastard, how many have you killed?'

Fred says, '17.'

So the coppers spend weeks digging up his house – and find 25 bodies. They go back to Fred and say, 'You bastard, you told us you killed 17.'

And Fred says, 'Yeah, but I'm a builder. It was only an estimate.'

## Leave the lights off

A guy on a date parks his car and gets his girlfriend in the back seat. They make love, and the girl wants to do it again almost instantly. They end up doing it a second, a third and a fourth time, until the bloke needs a rest and asks his girlfriend to excuse him as he needs to take a leak.

While out of the car, he notices a man a few yards away changing a flat tyre. He walks over and says, 'Listen, my girlfriend's over there in my car and I've already given it to her four times and she still wants more. If you give her one for me, I'll change your tyre.'

The lucky motorist readily agrees, climbs into the vehicle and begins shagging the insatiable girl. While he is banging away in the doggy position, a policeman shines a torch through the window.

'What do you think you're doing there?' he asks the man, who replies, 'I'm making love to my wife.' The policeman looks bemused and says, 'Why don't you do it at home?'

The man answers, 'Well, I didn't know it was my wife until you shone the torch on her.'

## Cold comfort

A married couple receive a bank statement saying they have a huge overdraft. They also receive a final demand for the gas bill, so they agree to save money. That evening, while watching TV, the man gets up and tells his wife that he's off down the pub. Outraged, the wife informs him that he has no right to go off to the pub and leave her at home when they need to economize.

The husband nods and tells his wife to put her coat on.

Surprised, the wife asks, 'Why? Are we going out together?'

'No,' he says. 'I'm turning the heating off.'

## Like ships that pass in the night

After months of plucking up courage, Tony decides to take a parachute jump. But after leaping out of the tiny Cessna aircraft, he pulls the ripcord ... and nothing happens. Alarmed, he pulls his reserve chute cord – and again, nothing happens. As he's plummeting towards earth – and certain death – he spots another man shooting upwards at rapid speed.

'Do you know anything about parachutes?' cries Tony, as the man passes him.

'No,' comes the reply. 'Do you know anything about gas cookers?'

## Crocodile does tricks

A bloke walks into a bar with a crocodile. Predictably, most of the patrons scarper and the barman complains. But the owner of the croc says, 'No worries, mate, watch this.'

Picking up a bottle, he smashes it over the croc's head. No reaction, other than a wag of the head. The bloke then gets his cock out and puts it in the croc's mouth, but again the croc just wags its head. Then a fellow punter asks if he can try it.

'Help yourself, mate,' says the owner.

The punter proceeds to smash a bottle over the croc's head and then put his cock in its mouth. The croc just gives its usual response. Word spreads and several blokes try it. Then an old biddy walks up and asks for a go.

'Can I just make one request, though?' she says to the owner.

'Ask away,' he replies.

'Don't hit me so hard with the bottle.'

# Revenge is a dish best eaten cold

One day a 12-year-old boy walks into a brothel, dragging a dead frog behind him and says, 'Hello, I'd like a girl for the night.'

The madam says, 'I'm afraid you're too young for one of my girls.'

So he gets out his wallet and gives her £200, to which she says, 'She'll be waiting for you upstairs.'

The boy says, 'She's got to have active herpes.'

'But all my girls are clean!'

So out comes another £200. The madam says, 'Okay.'

So the boy goes upstairs, dragging the dead frog. Half an hour later, he comes back down, still dragging the dead frog. By now the madam is curious, and asks, 'Why did you come in here dragging a dead frog and asking for a girl with active herpes?'

'Well,' he says, 'when I get home, I'll fuck the baby-sitter, and she'll get it. Then, when my parents get home, Dad will drive her home and have sex on the way, so he'll get it. Later, Mum and Dad will make love, and she'll get it. Then, when Dad has gone to work, the milkman will come round and fuck my mum, and he'll get it. And he's the bastard who killed my frog!'

## Overheard ... at the hospital

**TWs, cutters and skulls:** Various occupants of the casualty waiting room – time wasters, suicides and anorexics.

**Fubar:** 'Fucked up beyond all recognition'. Usually as a result of an MVA, or a motor vehicle accident.

**Fubar bundy:** A patient who would be better off dead – 'Fucked up beyond all recognition, but unfortunately not dead yet.'

**Taps punter:** A most ignorant patient – Mr Thick As Pig Shit.

**Houseplants:** First-year doctors.

**Ash cash:** The £30 fee given to doctors for filling out a cremation form.

**FLK:** Commonly heard in maternity wards. FLKs are babies who don't look right, or funny-looking kids.

**Sad, mad and bad:** Psychiatric patients – manic depressives, the clinically insane and those with personality disorders.

**Slimmers:** Aids sufferers.

## A dream come true

For quite some time, a man has lived next door to a beautiful young girl.
He curses his lack of confidence, as he's never said more than hello to the
fantastic creature on his doorstep. Then one day, as he returns from work, the
girl appears at her front door wearing a flimsy negligée and beckons him over.
As she slides her arms around his neck, it's obvious she's coming on to him,
and the man gets increasingly hot under the collar.

All of a sudden she looks up.

'Inside, quickly,' she whispers urgently, 'I can hear someone coming.'

Blind with lust, he follows her indoors where she strips off and stands in front
of him, stark naked.

'So, honey,' she coos, 'what do you think my best attribute is?'

'Well,' the man stammers, 'It's ... er ... got to be your ears.'

The woman frowns at him incredulously.

'My ears?' she gasps. 'But why? Have you ever seen such flawless skin? Such
pert breasts? Have you ever set eyes upon such a firm backside?'

'No – I agree,' says the man.

The woman shakes her head 'And yet you say my ears ...'
'Well it's like this,' he explains, 'When we were outside, you said you could hear someone coming.'
'So?' she demands.
The man gulps. 'Well, that was me.'

# Drac attack

One day Dracula is walking down the street, when suddenly ten tons of smoked salmon sandwiches, bread rolls, pitted olives, chicken wings, chipolatas, tomato salad, pizza slices and crisps descends on him from a great height, knocking him to the ground.
'Oh no!' he gasps with his dying breath, 'It's Buffet the Vampire Slayer!'

# Rationing

Little Johnny is delivering newspapers one morning. He knocks at the door of Mrs Smith, and tells her that her bill is due.
'That'll be £5 please,' he says.
'I'm a little short of cash,' Mrs Smith says. 'But if you want to step in here I can pay you in sex.'
Johnny steps in, and shuts the door. Mrs Smith unzips his pants, pulls them down and is faced by the biggest cock she's ever seen. She lies down on the hall carpet and is bemused to see Johnny pulling something from his jacket pocket. He takes a handful of big washers out, and slips them onto his massive cock.
'You don't have to do that,' Mrs Smith says. 'I can take all of it.'
Johnny looks down at Mrs Smith and says, 'Not for £5 you can't.'

# The old ones are the best

A man walks into a pub with a lump of tarmac under his arm.
'A pint please, landlord,' he says, 'and one for the road.'

# Are they related?

What have Kermit the Frog and Henry the VIII got in common?
They both have the same middle name.

## Taking things literally

Three men are sitting in a pub, bored shitless. The first bloke says to the others, 'Right, let's play a game. When we get home tonight, we have to do the first thing our wives tell us to.'

The other two agree, and they all decide to meet up the next evening to discuss the results. When they are all back in the pub, the first man tells his tale. 'I got home and the wife was washing up, so I decided to help her. I started drying the dishes, and I dropped one. "That's right," she said, "smash the place up." So I got a sledgehammer and destroyed the entire house. Now she's divorcing me and I've been charged with wilful destruction.'

'You think that's bad,' the second man says. 'When I got home, I fell asleep on the sofa, dropped a fag and scorched the carpet. The wife came in and said, "Oh good, burn the whole house down." So I torched the place. I'm being divorced, and I'm also up for arson.'

'You lucky bastard,' the third man says. 'When I got home, my wife was in bed, so I climbed in next to her. I was feeling a bit amorous, and I started tickling her downstairs. She said to me, "You can cut that out for a start." Anybody want a toupée?'

## Does he work at Paddington?

Jimmy was applying for a job as a switch operator on the railroad. The chief engineer was conducting the interview.

'What would you do,' asked the engineer slowly, 'If the Northern Express was heading north on Track 1 and the Southern Central was heading south on Track 1?'

Jimmy frowned. 'Well,' he began, thoughtfully. 'I'd call my brother.'

The chief engineer looked at him for a second.

'Why would you call your brother?' he asked.

'He's never seen a train wreck before,' said Jimmy.

## The nice gesture

Two men are sitting on a riverbank, fishing. Suddenly, they look up and see a funeral procession going over the bridge. One of the men takes off his cap and solemnly holds it over his heart.

'That was a nice gesture,' says the other man.

'Oh,' replies the first, 'it's the least I can do. We were married 25 years.'

## Rest in puss

Little Tim was in the garden filling in a hole when his neighbour peered over the fence. Interested in what the cheeky-faced youngster was up to, he politely asked, 'What are you up to there, Tim?'

'My goldfish died,' replied Tim tearfully, without looking up, 'and I've just buried him.'

The neighbour frowned. 'That's an awfully big hole for a goldfish, isn't it?'

Tim patted down the last heap of earth. 'Well,' he replied, 'That's because he's inside your fucking cat.'

## Overheard ... in Canada

**Beaver fever:** Nasty little digestive illness caused by bacteria living in freshwater mountain streams.

**Cabin fever:** Nasty little mental illness caused by having to spend too long indoors during the dark, freezing and utterly tedious winter.

**Fruit leather:** Dried fruit purée pressed in to fairly unpleasant thin sheets. Much appreciated by hiking types.

**Great explosion:** The greatest moment in Canadian history, when a French ship loaded with TNT collided with another ship in Halifax harbour, producing the biggest man-made non-nuclear explosion ever.

**Mukluks:** The height of fashion in the snowy wastes – sealskin moccasins or boots, made by the Inuit.

**Newfie:** A resident of Newfoundland, a place second only to Iceland in the list of unimaginative names.

**No-see-um:** Any irritating insect that snacks on people.

**Ogopogo:** A monster that is supposedly resident in Okanagen Lake. Although, curiously, no one has ever seen it.

**Screech:** Strong and quite vile rum previously made in Newfoundland; now widely available, but in pathetic diluted form.

**Sourdough:** Someone who has had the dubious privilege of spending an entire year in the north of the country.

**Spelunking:** Mucking about in caves.

**Steamies:** Not the kind of films Canadians watch during the long, dark nights, but a Quebec expression for hot dogs.

## White as a sheet

As the congregation settled into the pews, the preacher rose to the lectern with a red face. 'Someone in this congregation,' he began gravely, 'has spread a rumour that I belong to the Ku Klux Klan.'

As whispering spread around the hall, the padre continued.

'This is a horrible lie – one I am embarrassed about and one which a Christian community cannot tolerate. I ask the party who did this to stand and ask forgiveness from God.'

No one moved, and the preacher continued. 'Do you not have the nerve to face me and admit this is a falsehood? Remember, you will be forgiven and in your heart you will feel glory.'

Again all was quiet. Then, slowly, a drop-dead gorgeous blonde rose from the third pew. Her head was bowed and voice quivered as she spoke.

'Reverend, there has been a terrible misunderstanding. I never said you were a member of the Klan.'

'Oh?' said the Father, 'So what did you say?'

The blonde chewed her lip sadly. 'I simply mentioned to a couple of friends that you were a wizard under the sheets.'

# The four parrots

Feeling very lonely because her husband had died the year before, a Jewish lady decides to buy a pet to keep her company. So, she goes to her local pet shop and explains her situation to the shop manager.

'I've got just the thing for you,' he says. 'This is Bella, a female parrot – she will chat sweetly to you all day.'

The Jewish lady is delighted and buys the bird. When she gets the parrot home she says, 'Come on, Bella – say something.'

Bella says 'My name is Bella. I like to fuck and I want some sex!'

The old lady is shocked and nearly passes out. She leaves it for an hour or so and approaches the parrot once more. But no luck: 'My name is Bella and I want to fuck!'

The lady decides enough is enough and plans to return the parrot immediately. However, just as she's about to leave, the local rabbi comes round. She explains her bad luck with the parrot.

'Don't worry,' says the rabbi, 'I've got three parrots at home and I've taught them so well that all they do is pray all day! Let me take Bella to them and they'll make her a good parrot.'

The widow agrees and so the rabbi leaves with Bella. He gets home and tells his parrots, 'This is Bella, she is bad, you must teach her to be good.'

Bella shouts, 'My name is Bella, I like to fuck and I want sex now.'

The rabbi's parrots look at each other and one shouts, 'I told you if we prayed long enough ...'

# Beer call

Returning from an exhausting day at work, a man plops down on the couch in front of the TV.

'Hey, darling,' he shouts to his wife, 'Get me a beer before it starts.'

His wife sighs and fetches him a beer. 'Actually,' says the man as she's walking away, 'I'll probably need another beer before it starts.'

She looks cross, but fetches another tinny and slams it down next to him. But after gulping down both beers, the husband is still not satisfied. 'Quick, get me another beer,' he says. 'It's going to start any minute!'

'No, I won't!' screams the furious wife back. 'Is that all you're going to do tonight? Drink beer and sit in front of that TV? You're nothing but a lazy, drunken, fat slob – and furthermore...'

'Damn,' sighs the man. 'It's started.'

# Sporting chance

Finishing his ploughing run early one evening, a farmer heads home – hoping to spend time with his gorgeous young wife. But, upon entering the farmhouse, he hears panting and moaning coming from the bedroom. Furious, he grabs his 12-bore shotgun, edges his way upstairs and inches the bedroom door open. There, sure enough, is his young farmhand, pumping away on top of his wife. Enraged, the farmer bursts in waving his shotgun. His wife screams and runs away in panic – leaving the terrified farmhand, shaking on his knees, in the middle of the floor.

The farmer presses his gun at the lad's testicles.

'Boy!' he barks, 'I'm going to blow these off. Anything to say?'

'Please!' stutters the young buck. 'Give me a chance!'

The farmer narrows his eyes. 'Okay,' he snarls. 'Swing 'em.'

# The spoilt child

A man takes his spoilt son to the fair on his birthday, and promises he can have whatever he wants for the duration of the day.

'Dad, Dad, can I go on the big wheel?' the boy whines, and the father duly takes him on the big wheel. This is followed by the bumper-cars, the waltzer, three hot dogs and a toffee apple.

'Dad, Dad, let me have a go on the shooting range,' the child then asks. The boy wins a teddy, and demands to name it whatever he wants. Dad agrees, and the boy shouts, 'I'll call him Wanker!' For the rest of the day, he talks to Wanker in a loud voice, much to the shame of his father.

As they're getting into the car to go home, the father accidentally leaves the teddy on the roof of the car. As they set off, the bear falls onto the road.

'Daddy, Daddy, Wanker's off!' the little boy cries, to which the old man says, 'God, son, I know it's your birthday – but I think you've had quite enough for one day.'

# He had a hunch ...

Quasimodo, the Hunchback of Notre Dame, returns home from a hard day ringing the cathedral bells – and finds his wife standing in the kitchen with a wok.

'Fantastic,' he says, 'Is it Chinese tonight, Esmerelda?'

'Oh, no,' she says, 'I'm ironing your shirt.'

# Taking the piss

A man is sitting in the pub having a quiet pint when a gremlin comes in and asks for a half. He downs his drink quickly, then runs along the bar, sticks his head in the man's pint and shakes it around. The man is bemused, but continues to drink as the gremlin returns to his seat. The little beastie orders a second and third half and after each one does exactly the same thing. The man finally loses his patience and grabs the gremlin by the scruff of the neck. 'If you stick your head in my pint one more time, I'll rip your dick off!' shouts the angry drinker.

'Ain't got one,' says the gremlin.

The man looks confused. 'If you haven't got a cock, how do you piss?' he asks the gremlin.

'Like this,' says the gremlin, and sticks his head in the man's pint, shaking it around.'

# Overheard ... at the fairground

**Belly joint:** A rigged game or attraction where the operator manipulates the results by subtly applying pressure to the mechanics with his stomach. As in 'Don't bother to play the roulette wheel. It's a belly joint.'

**The blow-off:** An encore offered to customers at the end of the main attraction. And always at an extra cost to them.

**The chump-heister:** The ubiquitous Ferris wheel.

**A fifty-miler:** A fairground ride operator who never moves too far from his main pitch. Used as an insult by travelling fairground workers.

**To gaff:** To rig a game or slot machine so no one ever wins.

**The grinder:** The worker who stands outside an attraction and yells the same thing over and over again in an attempt to lure customers to his pitch.

**Marks:** Customers.

**Pickled punks:** Human foetuses joined together and displayed in jars of formaldehyde. Usually billed as 'Live Siamese Twins' at freak shows.

**Signal 40:** The codeword used when someone throws up on a ride. As in, 'Send a cleaner to the dodgems, We've got a signal 40.'

**Slum:** Rubbish prizes at an attraction that actually cost less than the cost of the game.

**The town clowns:** Policeman assigned to beat duty at the fair.

**The whoop-de-doo:** The most thrilling ride in the fairground. 'The Marks will be off the dipper in a minute. They're just coming up to the whoop-de-doo at the end.'

## The secret of a long life

Sat on a park bench, a small boy is munching one chocolate bar after another.
After seeing him starting on his sixth, a man on the bench across from him
shakes his head.

'Son,' tuts the gentleman, 'Eating all that chocolate isn't good for you. It will
give you acne, rot your teeth and make you fat.'

The small boy looks back at him. 'My grandfather lived to be 107,' he replies.

The man nods sagely. 'But did your grandfather eat six candy bars at a time?'

The boy looked at him. 'No,' he said, 'He just minded his own fucking business.'

## Fountains of Wayne

An Essex girl goes to the local social benefits office to claim her family
allowance, and tells the officers that she has ten children.

'Wow!' says the clerk. 'What are their names?'

'Wayne, Wayne, Wayne, Wayne, Wayne, Wayne, Wayne, Wayne, Wayne and
Wayne,' the woman answers, smiling proudly.

The man looks at her dubiously. 'Really?' he says. 'So what if you want them
to come in from playing outside?'

'That's easy – I just shout Wayne and they all come running,' answers
the woman.

The clerk is not convinced. 'And what if you want them to come to the table
for dinner?' he asks.

'Again,' says the claimant, 'I just shout 'Wayne – dinner's ready!''

'But wait a minute,' says the man, his brow furrowed. 'What if you just want
*one* of them to do something?'

'That is slightly more difficult,' says the woman, nodding. 'Then I have to use
their last names.'

## The thoughtful wife

George the postman was on the final day of his job after 35 years of serving
the same neighbourhood, come rain or shine. At his first house, he was
greeted by the entire family applauding him, and sent on his way with a
healthy gift envelope. At the second house, he was presented with a case of
fine wine, at the third he left with a box of Havana cigars.

At the fourth house, George was greeted by a beautiful blonde in a baby-doll
nightie, who took him by the hand upstairs to the bedroom and treated him

to the best sex of his life. Afterwards she led him to the kitchen and cooked him breakfast.

As the stunning woman poured the coffee, the postie noticed a £1 coin next to his cup. 'What's the money for?' he asked.

'Oh,' the woman replied. 'Last night I told my husband that today was your last day, and I asked him what we should give you as a special treat. He said, "Fuck him. Give him a pound." The breakfast was my idea.'

## Beetlemania

A man is sitting at home watching TV late one night when there's a knock at the front door. The man angrily answers the door to find a 6-ft stag beetle standing on the step. After he asks the beetle what the hell he thinks he is playing at calling at such a late hour, the creature lays into him with a series of vicious kicks and punches. It then walks away, while the man crawls back inside his house and calls an ambulance.

At the hospital the man is reluctant to tell the doctor how he came about his injuries, but eventually relates the incredible tale of the stag beetle, expecting to be laughed at.

To his surprise the doctor is sympathetic, explaining to the man that there is a nasty bug going about.

# Spelling test

A young woman visits the doctor for a breast examination. When he sees her he is surprised to see an 'O'-shaped mark on her chest.

'Oh', she explains. 'That's from my boyfriend's Oxford University jumper. He likes to wear it when we have sex and the crest rubs against my skin.'

A couple of weeks later, another girl is in for a breast examination. She whips her top off, and there is a 'C' in the middle of her chest. The doctor raises an eyebrow while the girl explains that her lover likes to wear his Cambridge University jumper during sex.

Weeks later, a third girl comes in for an examination and she has a 'W' on her chest. 'Ah!' cries the doctor. 'Let me guess, you have a boyfriend at Warwick?'

'No,' smiles the girl. 'I've got a girlfriend at Manchester.'

# Dangerous discharge

A woman who's pregnant with triplets is walking down the street, when out of the bank runs a robber. In the ensuing gunfight, he shoots the woman three times in the stomach.

At the hospital the woman is told that her babies are unhurt, and she gives birth a month later to two girls and a boy. All goes swimmingly for 16 years, until one day the mother finds one daughter crying. 'What's wrong, dear?' she asks concerned.

'Well I was doing a wee and a bullet came out!'

'Oh ...' says the woman, relieved, and proceeds to tell her daughter of that fateful day 16 years ago.

A month passes and the second daughter comes to her mum crying, with the same problem. 'Not to worry', says the mum. 'I'll explain it to you ...'

Another month passes and the boy comes in very concerned and close to tears. The kindly mother takes the boy in her arms and asks him, 'Were you doing a wee and a bullet came out, my love? Because if you did, it's okay.'

'Nah,' replies the lad. 'I was having a wank and I shot the dog!'

# Upper-class twit of the year

Tarquin the upper-class git comes across a beautiful naked woman lying in the forest with her legs spread wide open. Not believing his luck, he approaches her and asks her if she's game.

The woman replies 'Yes', so he shoots her.

# Too-late tailor

Joe is being plagued by terrible headaches. One day, after years of suffering, he decides to see a migraine specialist. The doctor tells Joe to strip, inspects him all over, and announces that he's found the cause of his problem.

'Your testicles are pressing against the base of your spine,' says the medic. 'The pressure builds up, and you get an excruciating headache.'

Joe is appalled. 'Tell me, doctor, is there anything I can do about it?' he asks. 'I'm afraid I have bad news. The only answer is to get rid of the testicles,' says the doctor.

Joe considers the pros and cons of a life without balls and sex – but then he thinks about the agony of his daily headaches, and without too much difficulty decides to go for the snip.

He comes round from the operation and leaves the hospital. Walking along the street, he smiles as he realizes that the pain has completely disappeared. To celebrate, he decides to treat himself to some new clothes, so he makes his way to a top tailor to get fitted.

Inside the tailor's, he asks to see a pair of trousers. The tailor looks at Joe and says, 'You'll need a 36-inch waist, 33-inch inside leg.'

Joe is amazed at the accuracy of the tailor's eye, and asks for a shirt. 'That'll be a 42-inch chest, 16-inch neck,' the tailor says, and Joe is once again stunned by his accuracy.

Finally, all that is left is a pair of underpants. '36?' guesses the tailor incorrectly.

'No, sorry, I'm a 34,' Joe says. 'I've worn a 34 since I was 18.'

'This is not possible,' frowns the tailor. 'If a man of your size wore a size 34, the pants would press his testicles into the base of his spine, causing the most horrific headaches.'


# Two men in a boat

After weeks of floating adrift in a tiny boat, two men are forlornly watching the sea for signs of a ship. All of a sudden a huge hand emerges from the water near the boat. It leans all the way over to the left, and then all the way over to the right. Then it happens again – moving all the way over to the left then back to the right, before slipping silently beneath the surface. The men look at each other.

'Christ,' says one. 'Did you see the size of that wave?'

## Eskimo humour

An Eskimo is out for a drive one day when his car breaks down and he is
forced to call out the Alaskan AA. The Eskimo stands in the howling wind and
waits for the mechanic to arrive. When the mechanic reaches the broken car,
he sets to work, looking under the bonnet until he locates the problem.
He looks up at the Eskimo and says, 'You've blown a seal, mate.'
To which the Eskimo hastily replies, 'No I haven't! That's just frost on
my moustache.'

## The talking tortoise

A lonely man goes to the pet shop to buy an animal for some company.
'I have the perfect pet for you,' says the owner. 'It's an amazing tortoise: it
will do almost everything – and it even talks.'
'I'll take it,' says the man.
Later on that evening, the man decides to put his pet's skills to the test.
'Tortoise, go down to the shop and buy me a paper!' he cries, placing the
tortoise on the floor outside the living room.
A year later, the man is still watching TV when he remembers his tortoise.
'Bloody hell! That tortoise is so slow I'd best go and look for him.' He steps out
of his front door and, to his surprise, nearly steps on his missing pet.
'You're so bloody slow, you've been gone for nearly a year. Where's my paper?'
To which the disgruntled tortoise replies, 'Well if you're going to be like that,
I won't go!'

## We love you really, Peter

Bill died and went to heaven, where he was met at the gates by an angel who
led him to a large warehouse. Each wall was lined with thousands of clocks.
'Each clock represents a person's lifetime,' said the angel. The hands on one of
the clocks suddenly spun around furiously, taking an hour off the time.
'What was that?' asked Bill curiously.
The angel explained that each time someone acted like a wanker, an hour was
knocked off their life.
The pair carried on walking, then Bill asked the angel if he could possibly see
the famous pop star Peter Andre's clock.
'Oh, yes,' said the angel. 'But you'll have to come into the office. We've been
using it as fan during this hot spell.'

## He's been stung before

One day Jane met Tarzan in the jungle. She was very attracted to him and during her questions about his life she asked him what he did for sex.

'What's that?' he asked. She explained to him what sex was and he said 'Oh, I use a hole in the trunk of a tree.'

'Tarzan, you have it all wrong,' she says horrified, 'but I will show you how to do it properly.'

She took off her clothes, laid down on the ground and spread her legs wide. 'Here,' she said, 'You must put it in here.'

Tarzan removed his loincloth, stepped closer and then gave her an almighty kick in the crotch. Jane rolled around in agony. Eventually she managed to gasp, 'What the hell did you do that for?'

'Just checking for bees,' said Tarzan.

# Bad exchange

A Japanese man walks into a currency exchange in Trafalgar Square and hands 10,000 yen over the counter. The woman smiles and hands him back £70. The following week, he again walks in and puts down 10,000 yen – but this time the teller only gives him £60.

'Why less this week?' he asks the teller.

The lady smiles and says, 'Fluctuations.'

The Japanese man storms out, and just before slamming the door, turns around and says, 'Well, fluc you Blittish, too.'

# The well-hung fly

While out shopping one day, a woman spots her husband cheating with another woman in a restaurant. Waiting until he returns home, the wife pretends everything is normal – cooking his dinner, ironing his shirts and waiting for him to go up to bed. As soon as he is asleep, she stalks into the bedroom, pulls off the covers and cuts off his penis with a bread knife. As the husband wakes up, screaming, the wife panics and runs downstairs, still clutching the severed member in her bloody hand. Suddenly realizing the consequences of her actions, she leaps into the family saloon and speeds off into the night.

It's not long before she skids over the roundabout and onto the nearby motorway. Accelerating up to 90 mph, she soon attracts the attention of a police car and decides she has to get rid of the evidence. Opening the sunroof, she throws the flaccid organ out – only to see it bounce of the cop car windscreen.

'I think this woman must be a nutter,' says the police sergeant, hot in pursuit. 'I don't know about that,' says second officer, 'But did you see the size of the cock on that fly?'

# While the cat's away ...

Early one morning, a milkman is doing his rounds. He goes up to one of the houses and knocks on the door to collect the milk money. A small boy answers the door smoking a huge Havana cigar, swigging from a bottle of lager, his arm around what appears to be a call girl.

The milkman looks at the small boy and asks, 'Is your mum or dad in?'

The little lad replies, 'Does it look like it?'

# Man finds topless woman

Unemployed for a number of years, Barry finally lands a job working for the local railway company. One night he meets up with some friends in the pub.

'So how's the new job, Barry?' asks one of his mates.

'Brilliant,' he replies. 'The other day I was out working when I found a woman tied to the tracks. I untied her, took her back to my place for a cup of tea and ended up shagging her all night. It was fantastic! Missionary, doggy-style, wheelbarrow – you name it, we did it.'

'Yeah?' enquires one of his friends. 'But was she good-looking?'

'I dunno,' sighs Barry. 'I couldn't find the head.'

## Overheard ... on Baywatch

**Beat off:** An unfortunate expression for the sort of lifeguard who would rather let a senior citizen drown than get his trunks wet.

**Blitz:** The type of heroic rescue that involves fishing several panicked actors from the briny at once.

**Buffasorus:** Bloke who has pumped enough iron to produce a top-ten physique.

**Didge:** Parking area that requires no pay 'n' display small change fumbling.

**Climbing the ladder:** Swimming 'straight up' – a technique that shows you're hopeless in the water and will need rescuing soon.

**Rubber ducky:** Unlike a bathtime plaything, this is a boat with an outboard motor – handy in stiff currents rarely found in the tub.

**Sky genie:** A device with loads of ropes and pulleys, only useful for rescuing idiots stuck on cliffs.

**Dumped:** Knocked over by a boisterous wave.

**Towelside manner:** A lifeguard's ability to get fresh with sunbathing women.

**Tumble dry:** To get knocked over and rolled up on the beach by a wave that's bigger than you.

## Go, sister!

Two nuns are sitting in the traffic waiting for the lights to change when suddenly a vampire appears in front of them.

'Oh sister, what shall we do?' stammers the younger nun.

'Do not worry,' came the reply. 'Show him your cross.'

The younger nun winds down the windscreen and yells, 'Fuck off, you little twat!'

## The truth dawns

This woman's husband had been slipping in and out of a coma for several months, yet she had stayed by his bedside every single day. One day, when he came to, he motioned for her to come nearer. As she sat by him, he whispered to her, his eyes full of tears. 'My dearest, you have always been with me. All through the bad times: when I got fired, you were there to support me. When my business failed, you were there. When we lost the house, you stayed right here. When my health started failing, you were still by my side. You know what?'

'What dear?' she gently asked, smiling, as her heart began to fill with warmth.

'I think you're bad luck.'

# He can hold his drink

In their local pub, a man and a woman are having a pint. When the man goes to the toilet, another man sits in his seat and starts chatting to the woman. 'I'm going to shag you here and now,' proclaims the man.

'No you won't – I'll get my husband,' she replies.

'And then,' continues the man, 'I'm going to strip you naked and lick your body.'

'When my husband gets back, he'll kill you!' she warns.

'And once that's over with, I'm going to fill your pussy up with beer and then drink it through a straw!'

'Right, that does it!' she yells, running off to get her husband. A few minutes later, she returns with him and explains what the pest had said.

'He said he was going to shag me,' cries the lady while her husband takes off his coat. 'And then he said he wanted to lick my naked body,' she sobs as her husband rolls up his sleeves. 'And worst of all, he said he was going to fill my pussy with beer and drink it all up through a straw!'

At this, the man rolls his sleeves down, puts his coat back on and heads for the door. 'What are you doing?' protests the woman.

To which the man replies, 'I'm not fighting anyone who can drink that much beer!'

# The Pope's four conditions

The day arrived in the Vatican for the Pope's annual physical – and the Holy See were dismayed to hear he'd been diagnosed with a rare form of testicular cancer. A genito-urinary specialist was called and, after examination, told him the only cure is to have sex. After some thought, the Pope licked his dry lips and spoke. 'I agree,' he says. 'But under four conditions.'

As uproar broke out, a single voice cried out from the hubbub: 'And what are these conditions?'

The room stilled. There was a long pause, before the Pope croaked, almost inaudibly: 'First, the girl must be blind, so she cannot see who I am.'

The cardinals nodded.

'Second, she must be deaf, so that she cannot hear who I am. And third she must be dumb so that if somehow identifies me, she can tell no one.'

The was another pregnant pause.

'And the fourth condition?' a Cardinal piped up.

The Pope grinned. 'Big tits.'

## Pet lovers

Harry was hired to play his trumpet on the score of a movie, and was
especially thrilled because he got to take two long solos. After the sessions,
which went wonderfully, Harry couldn't wait to see the finished product and
asked the producer when he could catch the film. A little embarrassed, the
producer explained that the music was for a porno flick that would be out
in a month, and he told Harry where he could go to see it.

A month later Harry, with his collar up and wearing glasses, went to the
theatre where the picture was playing. He walked in and sat way in the back,
next to an elderly couple. The movie started, and it was the filthiest, most
perverse porno flick ever. Jerry couldn't believe it as group sex, S&M and
golden showers shot across the screen – and then, just when it couldn't get
any worse, a dog got in on the action. Quick as a flash, the dog has had sex
with all the women, in every orifice; and with most of the men.

Embarrassed, Harry turned to the old couple and whispered, 'I'm only here
for the music.'

The woman turned to Harry and whispered back, 'That's okay, we're just here
to see our dog.'

## The Devil's decision

A womanizer dies and goes to hell for his sins. He's greeted by the Devil, who
tells him he has the choice of three rooms for his eternal stay. Asking if he
can view them before he decides, the man is led to the first room.

He opens the door to discover a million people standing on their heads on a
concrete floor.

'I don't like the look of that,' says the man. 'I want to see the next room.'

So Satan leads him further. When they reach the second room, the man opens
the door to reveal a million people standing on their heads on a wooden floor.

'No, that's not for me either,' says the philanderer, shaking his head.

Eventually, they reach the final room, and the man peeks round the door to
find a million people standing knee-deep in shit, smoking fags and drinking
coffee. Despite the atrocious smell, he decides this is the best option and tells
the Devil of his decision.

But five minutes later, the devil returns, claps his hands and orders:

'Okay, you lot. Coffee break's over. Back on your heads!'

## Free ride

This nun's standing at a bus stop when a double-decker pulls up. As she gets on, the nun notices she's the only passenger on the bus, so she turns to the driver and asks, 'Could you do me a very special favour, Mr Driver?'

'If I can,' he replies.

'Well, the thing is, I have a serious heart problem and I want to have sex for the first time before I die.'

'Erm, okay,' answers the driver.

'There are two conditions, though,' continues the nun. 'Firstly, we can't do it if you're married, because I don't want to commit adultery. Secondly, it has to be anal sex, because I have to die a virgin.'

The bus driver gives a nod, so they clamber upstairs and get down to it. When it's all over, though, the driver's racked with guilt.

'I'm so sorry, Sister, but I have a terrible confession – I'm married with three kids.'

'Don't fret, Mr Driver,' replies the nun, sympathetically. 'I have a confession, too. I'm on my way to a fancy-dress party and my name's Kevin.'

## Overheard ... in the boxing ring

**Bodysnatching:** Landing punch after painful punch on an opponent's bruised and battered body.

**A Stiff, a Body, a Bum:** Not a very good boxer.

**A Jericho:** Massive, frightening and nicely timed blow which makes the victim come tumbling down.

**Sending the wicked:** Effective yet illegal tactic of punching someone in the cobblers.

**Showboating:** Showing off and playing to the crowd, without really doing the business.

**A rumble:** A truly memorable scrap.

**Rope-a-dope:** Canny tactic deployed by Muhammed Ali, involving exhausting an opponent by hanging about on the ropes.

**Suzy Q:** Rocky Marciano's nickname for distinctly unfriendly, yet prize–winning, right hand.

**Chuck a terrible:** Take a pounding, prepare for defeat then snatch the bout with a lucky knockout in the last round.

**Nothing under the left tit:** Sadly lacking in enthusiasm for the contest.

**Hit him in the Derby:** Give the guy a smack in the stomach.

# A man who loves his job

The mayor of a town hears that a local sewage worker has been working without a single day off in 25 years. Impressed, the Mayor decides such an excellent worker deserves a personal visit.

After being kitted out in the necessary waders, the Mayor meets the man down in the sewers, and asks him how he could do such an unpleasant job for so long.

'It's actually quite interesting,' says the man. 'For instance, you see that turd over there?'

The mayor squints into the murky waters. 'Yes?'

'Well, that's from the butcher's shop on the High Street,' says worker. 'You can tell from the bits of sawdust stuck to it.'

'That's amazing,' says the Mayor, genuinely impressed.

'And that brown trout over there,' says the man. 'You can tell from the smell of petrol that it's from the carsey in the local mechanics.'

'Unbelievable!' says the Mayor. 'You truly are a poo maestro. But what about the bum cigar over there?'

'Oh, that's easy' says the worker, following his gaze. 'It's from my house.'

'How do you know?' replies the leader of the city.

'Well,' says the man. 'It's got my sandwiches tied to it.'

# Unlucky Arthur

A travelling salesman is touring an area in deepest rural Wales, and stays the night at a farmhouse. After a fine meal with the farmer, the salesman turns to his kind host and asks if there's any possibility of renting some 'companionship' for the evening.

'Well,' mulls the farmer. 'I'm afraid there's not many women around here like that. But there's always Arthur ...'

'Oh?' says the salesman, intrigued. 'How much does he charge?'

'It'll cost you £10,' comes the reply.

The salesman thinks about this. 'Seems a bit expensive,' he says.

'Well,' says the farmer, 'The local magistrate takes out £4 because he doesn't approve of that sort of thing.'

'So that's £4 for him and £6 for Arthur,' says the salesman.

The farmer shakes his head. 'No, the local constable also takes £4 because he doesn't approve of that sort of thing.'

'Christ,' says the salesman. 'So the magistrate gets £4, the bobby £4 – that only leaves £2 for Arthur.'

'No – we have to pay Gareth and Dai to hold him down,' says the farmer. 'You see, Arthur doesn't approve of that sort of thing either.'

# The bells! The bells!

On hearing that her elderly grandfather had just passed away Jennie went straight round to visit her grandmother. When she asked how her grandpa had died, her gran explained 'He had a heart attack during sex on Sunday morning'

Horrified Jennie suggested that shagging at the age of 94 was surely asking for trouble.

'Oh no' her gran replied, 'We had sex every Sunday morning, in time with the church bells, in with the dings and out with the dongs.'

She paused, and wiped away a tear. 'If it wasn't for that damn ice cream van going past, he'd still be alive'.

# Laughter is the best medicine

What's grey, sits at the end of your bed and takes the piss?
A kidney dialysis machine.

## Ask a stupid question ...

The phone at the local hospital rang, and the duty medic picked it up to hear a man speaking frantically on the other end.' My wife is pregnant and her contractions are only two minutes apart!' he babbled.

'Is this her first child?' the doctor asked.

'No, you idiot!' the man shouted. 'This is her husband!'

## One-way street

An elderly man is driving down the M1 when his mobile rings. Answering it, he hears his wife on the other end.

'Albert,' she says, 'Please be careful when you're driving back. I just heard on the radio that there's a maniac on the M1. He's driving the wrong way!'

'It's not just one,' Albert replies, 'There's fucking hundreds of them!'

## Overheard ... on an oil rig

**Blowy and lumpy:** Don't go out without your anorak on, it's windy with high seas.

**Slop jockey:** The man with the tall, white hat, French accent and surly demeanor who makes the dinners.

**Fuck the dog:** To do as little as possible.

**Pusher:** Pretend to be busy – he's the drilling foreman.

**Dope:** Could be a drug, could be a dimwit, but instead it's a lubricant used on drill-pipe connections.

**Joint:** More suspicious narcotic terminology, this time describing a 40-ft piece of pipe.

**Donkey dick:** A large, black object in a rather amusing shape.

**Tripping:** Yes, you're out of your head, but through boredom, because tripping is putting lots of joints together.

**Fishing:** Irritating process of trying to retrieve something lost in a hole.

**Mud Man:** Not a member of top 1970s glam-rock outfit, but the bloke responsible for the mud pumped into a bore hole.

**Obvious, isn't it?**
What's 'ET' short for?
Because he has little legs.

# The memory man

Dave the scouser is touring the US on holiday and stops in a remote bar in the hills of Nevada. He's chatting to the bartender when he spies an old Indian sitting in the corner – complete with full tribal gear, long white plaits and wrinkled face.

'Who's he?'' asks Dave.

'That's the Memory Man,' says the bartender. 'He knows everything. He can remember any fact. Go and try him out.'

So Dave wanders over, and thinking he won't know about English football, asks: 'Who won the 1965 FA Cup Final?'

'Liverpool,' replies the Memory Man, instantly.

The tourist is amazed. 'Who did they beat?'

'Leeds,' comes the reply – again, quick as a flash.

'And the score?'

The wise brave does not hesitate: 'Two-one.'

Thinking that details may fox him, Dave tries something more specific.

'Who scored the winning goal?' he asks.

The Red Indian doesn't even blink: 'Ian St John.'

The Liverpudlian is flabbergasted and, returning home, he regales his relatives and friends with his tale. But it's not enough – and soon he's determined to return and pay his respects to this amazing man. Ten years later he's saved enough money, and returns to the US. After weeks of searching through the towns of Nevada, Dave finds the Memory Man in a cave in the mountains – older, more wrinkled, resplendent in his warpaint and headdress.

Humbled by this vision, the scouser steps forward, bows and greets the brave in the traditional native tongue: 'How.'

The Memory Man squints at him.

'Diving header in the six-yard box,' he says.

# Getting the jump on a bouncer

A man drives from Aberdeen to London for a night out. He is stopped at
the door of a very posh restaurant by an enormous bouncer, who tells him
he can't come in without a tie.

'But I've just driven all the way from Aberdeen!' the man moans. It's no use,
however – strictly no tie, no entry. So the man returns to his car and looks for
something that will make do. He finally finds some jump leads and fashions
himself a bootlace-style affair, then returns to the club.

'Can I come in now?' he asks. The bouncer looks him up and down and replies,
'I suppose so, but make sure you don't start anything.

# You'd have put the same word in

A young cleric is preparing to board a plane when he hears the Pope is on
the same flight.

'This is exciting,' he thinks, 'I've wanted to see the Pope in person.' He's
therefore even more surprised when the Pope sits down next to him, and
starts work on a crossword puzzle.

'This is fantastic,' thinks the young priest. 'I'm really good at crosswords.
Perhaps if the Pope gets stuck, he'll ask me for assistance.'

Almost immediately, the Pope turns to him. 'Excuse me,' he croaks, 'but do you
know a four letter word referring to a woman? It ends in '-unt'?'

Only one word leapt to the priest's mind. 'My goodness,' he thinks, beginning
to sweat. 'I can't tell the Pope that. There must be another word.'

Racking his brains, it finally hits him, and he turns to the Pontiff. 'I think the
word you're looking for is 'aunt'.' he says, relieved.

'Of course,' says the Pope. 'Hmm. You don't have any Tippex, do you?'

# The power of spinach

What happened when Jesus went to Mount Olive?
Popeye kicked the shit out of him.

# A fishy tale

Two parrots are sitting on a perch. One says to the other, 'Can you smell fish?'

# The lousy hunter

Cletus the slack-jawed redneck goes up to the mountains for a spot of bear hunting. On his first day, he spots a mighty grizzly, takes aim with his rifle, fires – and misses. A few seconds later, the bear comes up behind him and taps him on the shoulder.

'You're trying to kill me, aren't you?' he says to Cletus, and Cletus nods, terrified. 'Well,' says the bear, 'it's your choice – either I bugger you or I kill you.'

That night, with a very sore arse, Cletus heads into town and buys a bigger rifle. The next day, he returns to the woods and spots his grizzly. He aims, fires and misses again. The bear offers him the same choice, and the hunter is once again shafted by the beast.

Back in town, Cletus buys an even bigger rifle and returns once more to kill his quarry. Suddenly, he spots the bear and shoots. But a few seconds later, he feels a heavy claw tapping him on the shoulder.

'You're not really here for the hunting, are you?' says the bear.

THUD!
THUMP!
THUD!

## Six items or less

A newly wed couple had just moved into a new neighbourhood and were anxious to meet other people, so they decided to join their local church. They met up with the reverend, who told them, 'We're not interested in having any part-time undedicated members in our congregation. Belonging is a big commitment. So in order to test your resolve, I'm going to ask you two to give up sex for 30 days. After all, Jesus used to head out into the desert for 40 days at a time, so I don't think this is too much to ask. If you can pass this test, we'll let you in.'

So the couple agree and go home, They come back 30 days later and the reverend asks them, 'Well, how did it go?'

The husband replies, 'For the first few weeks we were okay. But I started getting pretty pent-up in the last half of the month. The final straw came on the 29th day. My wife dropped a head of lettuce on the floor and bent over to pick it up, and there I was, staring at her nice, firm ass sticking up at me. I mean, I couldn't help it – I threw up her skirt, got her down on the floor and we had wild, passionate sex right then and there.'

The reverend says, 'I'm sorry, but that means you will no longer be welcome in our church.'

'To hell with that!' said the husband. 'We'll no longer be welcome in Tesco's!'

## Superior firepower

A patrol of Iraqi soldiers are driving through the desert when the commander hears a voice from behind a sand dune shout, 'One British Special Forces soldier is worth a thousand Iraqi soldiers!'

The commander tells his officers to send ten men over the hill to sort him out. After sounds of a firefight, a voice shouts from behind the sand dune, 'One British Special Forces soldier is worth a thousand Iraqi soldiers!'

The commander then orders 100 men over the sand dune. After noises of a firefight, one wounded Iraqi soldier crawls back down the sand dune then says to his commander, 'It's a trap. There are two of them!'

## It's obvious, really

What do you call an Italian with a rubber toe?
Roberto.

## Too many questions

After 50 years of happy marriage to Lena, Ole becomes very ill and realizes that he will soon die. In bed one night, Ole turns to his wife.

'Lena', he asks. 'When I am gone, do you think you will marry another man?'

Lena gave it some thought. 'Well, yes', she said. 'Marriage has been good to me and I think that I surely will marry again.'

Ole was taken aback. 'Why Lena', he cried, 'Will you bring your new husband into our house?'

'This is a fine house', said Lena, 'Yes, I think we will live here.'

'But Lena', Ole gasped, 'Will you bring your new husband into our bed?'

Lena said 'Ole, you made this bed, a good strong bed. Yes! Sure I will bring my new husband into this bed.'

Ole gulped. 'But Lena', he said in a quite voice, '...You won't ... ah ... let your new husband use my golf clubs, will you?'

Lena smiled at her husband. 'Oh, Ole!' she grinned, misty-eyed. 'Of course he won't use your golf clubs! He is left-handed.'

## Slow food

A man and his wife are driving through the Welsh countryside when they came across a roadsign:

'Llanfairpwllgwyngyllgogerychwyrndrobwllllantysiliogogogoch.'

After the husband attempts to say it, his wife starts laughing – and quickly, the pronunciation soon becomes an argument. So much so, in fact, that they're still debating as they pull into a restaurant in town. As they're settling their bill, the wife can't help questioning the cashier.

'Excuse me, but would you mind settling an argument between my husband and me?' she asks. 'Could you pronounce the name of where we are? Only please do it very slowly.'

The cashier rolls her eyes, and leans forward.

'Liiiiiiiittttlllllleeeee Chhhheeefffff', she says.

## Armless

A man wakes up in a hospital bed after a terrible accident and cries, 'Doctor! Doctor! I can't feel my legs.'

The doctor comes over to the poor chap's bedside and says, 'Of course you can't. I've amputated both your arms.'

## Bring her in at two-thirty

One day, a man walks into a dentist's surgery and asks how much it costs to extract wisdom teeth.

'£80,' the dentist says.

'That's a ridiculous amount,' the man says. 'Isn't there a cheaper way?'

'Well,' the dentist says, 'if I don't use an anaesthetic, I can knock it down to £60.'

'That's still too expensive,' the man says.

'Okay,' says the dentist. 'If I save on electricity and wear and tear on the tools, and simply rip the teeth out with a pair of pliers I could get away with charging £20.'

'Nope,' moans the man. 'It's still too much.'

'Hmm,' says the dentist, scratching his head. 'If I let one of my students on work experience have a crack, I suppose I could charge a fiver.'

'Marvellous,' says the man. 'Book the wife in for next Tuesday.'

## Therapy?

A man walks into a pub and orders a drink. He necks it, takes out his cock, and pisses all over the bar. The landlord is furious and tells the man to get out. He apologises profusely, saying he doesn't know what came over him, and that he will see a psychiatrist and get help.

A week later, the man goes back into the pub, orders a drink, takes out his cock and pisses all over the bar. Again, the furious landlord tells him to get out, and again the man apologises, and says he will definitely get some help from a psychiatrist for his unusual condition. He then leaves.

The following week, the man comes in and the landlord stops him before he can order a drink.

'It's okay,' says the man, 'I've been in treatment with my psychiatrist. Everything's fine.'

The landlord decides to give the man one more chance, and pulls him a pint. The man drinks it, then gets his cock out and pisses all over the bar. The landlord is stunned.

'I thought you'd been to see a psychiatrist,' he says.

'I have,' the man replies.

'But you've just pissed all over my bar again,' the landlord says.

'I know,' says the man. 'But I don't feel guilty about it any more.'

## The black hole

While out walking in the country, a man comes across a hole. Curious, he finds a small pebble and tosses it into the hole. He hears no sound, so picks up a slightly bigger one and throws that into the blackness. Again, he hears no sound. He picks up an even bigger rock, throws it into the hole, and again listens at the opening for some sound. Again, there is only silence. Looking around for something really big to chuck into the apparently bottomless pit, he finds a huge boulder and hurls it into the hole.

As he is kneeling at the side of the hole waiting for some sound, a goat comes charging down the road towards him. He manages to scramble out of the way in the nick of time, and the goat falls down into the black hole.

A few moments later, a farmer comes across the hill and approaches the man. 'Have you seen a goat around here?' the farmer asks, and the man, somewhat embarrassed that the goat has fallen down the hole while he was right next to it, answers that he hasn't.

'That's odd,' says the farmer, 'It must be around here somewhere because I left it tied to an enormous boulder.'

## If your name's not down ...

A Man United fan dies on match day and goes to heaven in his Man United shirt. Arriving at the top of the ethereal staircase, he knocks on the pearly gates – and out walks St Peter in a City scarf.

'I'm sorry, mate,' says St Peter, 'No Man United fans in Heaven.'

'What?' exclaims the man, astonished.

'You heard, no Man United fans.'

'But, but ... I've been a good man,' replies the Man United supporter.

'Oh, really,' says St Peter. 'What have you done, then?'

'Well,' said the guy, 'A month before I died, I gave £10 to the starving children in Africa.'

'Oh,' says St Peter, 'Anything else?'

'Well, two weeks before I died I also gave £10 to the homeless.'

'Hmmm. Anything else?'

'Yeah. On the way home yesterday, I gave £10 to the Albanian orphans.'

'Okay,' said St. Peter, 'You wait here a minute while I have a word with the Boss.'

Ten minutes pass before St. Peter returns, and looks the fan straight in the eye. 'I've had a word with God and he agrees with me,' he says. 'Here's your £30 back – now fuck off.'

## Walk like a man

The ambitious coach of an all-girls athletics team decides to start using steroids in an attempt to improve his girls' dismal performance. After a few weeks, the team begins to whip all the others in their area, so the coach decides to increase the drug dosage, tasting glory for the first time in his short, undistinguished career.

The team continues to perform well and even looks like making the national finals. The coach thinks long and hard, and – seeing the shining gold medals in his mind's eye – he adds more steroids to the girls' diet.

The team goes mental, winning every event and qualifying for the finals. Then, the night before the big day, disaster strikes. Penelope, a 16-year-old hurdler comes to the coach's office.

'Coach,' she sobs, 'I have a problem. Dark, wiry hair's growing on my chest.'

'Oh my God!' the coach screams. 'How far down does it go?'

'To my balls,' Penelope says, 'which is another point I wanted to raise.'

## Discommunication

A very, very drunk man flops onto a bus seat next to a priest. His tie is stained, his face plastered with lipstick and a half-empty bottle of gin is sticking out of his trouser pocket. He opens his newspaper and starts reading, but after a few minutes turns to the priest and asks, 'Hey, Father, do you have any idea what causes arthritis?'

'Yes,' the priest replies sternly. 'It's caused by loose living, being with cheap, wicked women, drinking too much alcohol and having complete contempt for your fellow man.'

'Well, I'll be damned,' the drunk mutters, and returns to his paper. The bus carries on its way, and a few minutes later the priest, feeling guilty about what he has just said, nudges the man and apologizes to him.

'I'm very sorry,' says the holy man. 'I didn't mean to come on so strong. It was mean-spirited and inconsiderate of me. How long have you been suffering from arthritis?'

'I haven't,' says the drunk. 'I was just reading here that the Pope has.'

## The frog chorus

A tramp walks into a bar and orders a drink.

'I don't think you're going to be able to pay for that, are you?' says the barman.

'Okay,' says the tramp. 'If I promise to show you something you've never seen before, will you give me a drink?'

Reluctantly, the barman agrees, and the tramp pulls a hamster out of his pocket and puts it on the bar. The furry creature runs over to the piano and bangs out a brilliant version of Imagine.

'That was amazing,' admits the barman as he pulls the tramp's pint.

Once he's downed it, the tramp asks for another.

'I'll need another miracle in return,' says the barman. So this time the tramp pulls out a frog and puts it on the bar. The frog clears his throat and sings Bohemian Rhapsody.

At this point, a man sitting in the corner of the bar comes up and gives him £100 for the frog.

When he's gone, the barman says to the tramp, 'Blimey, that's cheap. You could have got much more.'

'It's okay,' replies the tramp. 'The hamster's a ventriloquist!'

## What are the odds on that?

Two men are trying to play a round of golf when they catch up with two
women. They watch with mounting frustration as the women manage to hit
every water hazard, bunker and piece of rough – without waving them through,
as golf etiquette requires. After two tedious hours of waiting, one of the men
decides enough is enough and walks over to ask them if he can play through.
He strides up the fairway, but halfway up stops suddenly and quickly returns.
'I can't do it', he says to his playing partner. 'One of those women is my wife,
and the other is my mistress! Maybe it'd be better if you went to talk to them.'
The second man agrees, but halfway there he stops and returns, just like
his colleague had done.
'What's up?' asks the first man.
'I tell you what', says the second man, smiling sheepishly. 'It's a small
world, isn't it?'

## Forget-me-not

Two elderly couples are enjoying a friendly conversation when one of the men
turns to the other.
'Arthur, I've been meaning to ask you', says the pensioner. 'How's your course
at the memory clinic going?'
'Outstanding', replies Arthur. 'They teach us all the latest psychological
techniques: visualisation, association and so on. It's made a huge
difference for me.'
'That's great', says his mate. 'What was the name of the clinic again?'
Arthur goes blank, then wrinkles his brow. 'Wait there, I can do this.' He closes
his eyes, and his lips move as he thinks to himself.
'What do you call that flower with the red petals and thorns?' he says, finally.
'You mean a rose', says his friend.
'Yes, that's it!' say Arthur, and turns to his wife. 'Rose, what was the name of
that clinic?'

## Miracle cure

After a nasty car accident, a man's wife slips into a coma. After spending weeks
at her bedside, the husband is summoned to the hospital by the excited staff.
'It's amazing', says the doctor, breathlessly. 'While bathing your wife, one of
the nurses noticed she responded to touching her breasts.'

The husband is very excited, and asks what he can do.

'Well,' says the doc. 'If one erogenous zone provokes a response, perhaps the others will too.'

So the husband goes alone into the room, where he slips his hand under the covers and began to massage her clit. Amazingly, the woman begins to move and even moan a little. The man tells the doctor, waiting outside.

'Excellent!' he said. 'If she responds like that, I think you should try oral sex.'

Nodding, the husband returns to the room – but within minutes the heart monitor alarms go off, and the medics pile into the room.

'What happened?' shouts the doctor, as he checks the prone woman's pulse.

'I'm not sure,' replies the man. 'I think she choked.'

# Tool time

Having heard from the jury, the judge asked the accused serial killer to stand.

'You have been found guilty of murdering your postman with a chainsaw,' he said, sternly.

'You lying bastard!' screamed a man in the gallery, leaping to his feet.

The judge stared in astonishment, before turning back to the killer to continue with his verdict: 'You are also guilty of killing a housewife with a hammer.'

'You miserable shit!' yelled the man, again leaping to his feet.

'Sir,' the judge said, 'I am seconds away from charging you with bringing the court into disrepute. Kindly explain your outrageous interruptions.'

'I lived next door to that bastard for 20 years,' the man snarled, 'and did he ever have a garden tool when I needed one?'

# Those aren't pillows!

Three guys check into a hotel, but the clerk tells them that, because the lodge is fully booked, they'll all have to share a bed. However, being completely exhausted, they decide to take it.

Next morning, the guy who slept on the left says, 'Wow, I had the weirdest, most vivid dream. I dreamt I was having a wank!'

The bloke on the right says, 'You too?'

The guy in the middle says, 'You're both disgusting. I had an ordinary dream. I dreamt I went skiing.'

## Tree hugger

Driving his car through the countryside, a middle-aged man spots a naked youth with his arms tied around the trunk of a tree. The driver slows and winds his window down and he hears the naked lad wailing for help. After looking around to check he's not getting into some sort of trap, he gets out of his car to investigate.

'Oh, thank God!' the young man cries. 'I've had a terrible day!'

'I can see that,' says the driver, noticing the bruises and whip-marks on the young man's back. 'What on earth happened to you?'

'Well,' moans the young man, 'I was driving along when I saw this young woman in a pair of cut-offs and a bra hitch-hiking. I stopped to give her a lift, and as soon as I jumped out to put her rucksack in the boot two enormous blokes jumped out of the undergrowth, stripped me, tied me up and beat me, stole all my belongings and drove off in my car.'

'Oh dear, gorgeous,' says the driver, unbuckling his belt. 'It's just not your day, is it?'

## Overheard ... cops in America

**To be in a state of adiosis:** To take leave of the world as the victim of a fatal car accident.

**Bag bride:** A prostitute with an appetite for crack.

**Make a canoe:** Perform an autopsy. This involves cutting open the body and removing the organs, so hollowing it out.

**Donorcycles:** Motorbikes. Bike crashes tend to kill by head injury, leaving organs conveniently intact for potential transplants.

**Finger wave:** Digitally checking a suspect's back package for drugs.

**Flight deck:** Hospital ward reserved for druggies who've gone bonkers.

**Maytag:** A prisoner who trades sexual favours for protection.

**Ray people:** Loonies who falsely confess to murders.

**Shoulder surfing:** Stealing a glance at someone's cashpoint details in order to plunder their account.

**Smurfing:** Illegally laundering high-denomination stolen notes into smaller denominations through countless transactions – a tedious job performed by minions known as smurfs.

# Divine intervention

A rabbi and a priest are involved in a bad car crash. Their vehicles are totally demolished but both clergymen are uninjured. After they crawl out of their wrecked cars, the rabbi sees the priest's collar.

'So,' says the rabbi, 'you're a priest. I am a rabbi. Just look at our cars. Both are completely demolished and you and I stand here unscathed. God must have intended for us to meet and become great friends and live together in peace for the rest of our days.'

'I agree with you totally,' says the priest. 'This must be a sign from God. You will be my closest friend for as long as we both may live.'

'Look at this,' the rabbi continues. 'Here is another miracle already. Look here in the back. A bottle of Mogen David wine, unbroken. Surely God wants us to seal our friendship with a drink.'

With this, he pops the cork, and hands the bottle to the priest, who takes several swigs and passes it back to the rabbi. But he just hands it back to the priest.

'Aren't you having any?' the priest asks.

'No,' the rabbi replies. 'I think I'll just wait for the police.'

# Twisting in the wind

After hearing that one of the patients in a mental hospital had saved another from a suicide attempt by pulling him out of a bathtub, the director reviews the rescuer's file and called him into his office.

'Mr James,' says the official, 'Your records and your heroic behaviour indicate that you're ready to go home. I'm only sorry that the man you saved later killed himself with a rope around the neck.'

'Oh, he didn't kill himself,' Mr James replied. 'I hung him up to dry.'

# Lucky eighteen

An Englishman, American, and Arabian were in a bar talking about their families. The Englishman said, 'I have ten kids at home and if I had another one I would have a soccer team!'

'Well,' said the American guy, 'I have 15 kids at home and if I had another one I would have a football team!'

'Well,' said the Arabic guy, 'I have 17 wives at home.' He paused, sipping at his drink. 'If I had another one I would have a golf course.'

## The three corpses

Three smiling corpses are lying in a morgue in Alabama, and a detective goes into the coroner's to find out the cause of death. The coroner points to the first dead man.

'This is Cletus,' he says. 'He died after winning $23 million on the state lottery.' He then moves onto the second smiling corpse. 'This is Bo,' the coroner says with a grin. 'He died having oral sex with Trudy-May.'

Finally he moves onto the last smiling corpse. 'This is Roscoe,' says the coroner. 'He died after being struck by lightning.'

'Well,' asks the detective. 'Why in the hell was he smiling?'

'Oh,' says the coroner. 'He thought he was having his picture taken.'

## What a blow!

After stumbling upon an lamp in his cellar, a old man tries to clean it and is astonished when a genie appears and grants him one wish. The pensioner thinks hard, then unselfishly decides that peace in the Middle East would help humanity more than any petty personal gain.

'Hmm,' says the genie. 'I think that's beyond even my powers. It's a conflict as old as time itself, with intractable religious, social and economical issues involved. Could you please choose again?'

The old man thinks for a moment then asks if just once, possibly, he could receive a blow job from his wife.

The genie looks at him coldly. 'Okay,' he says. 'When you say the word *peace*, do you mean ...'

## Thriller night

When does Michael Jackson know it's bedtime? When the big hand touches the little hand.

## Thanks fur the memories

One Saturday, a man and a woman walk into a very posh shop.

'Show the lady your finest mink!' the man demands. So the owner of the shop goes in the back and comes out with a full-length coat.

As the lady tries it on, the owner sidles up to the man and whispers, 'Ah, sir, that particular fur goes for £50,000.'

'No problem!' says the man. 'I'll write a cheque!'

'Very good, sir,' says the owner. 'You may come by on Monday to pick the coat up, after the cheque clears.' So the man and the woman leave.

On Monday, the man returns on his own. The owner's outraged. 'How dare you show your face in here? There wasn't a penny in your account.'

'Sorry,' grins the man, 'but I wanted to thank you for the most wonderful weekend of my life!'

## Home remedy

Young Timmy pricks his finger on a drawing pin at school, and calls out to his teacher that he need to soak it in some cider.

'Cider!' the teacher exclaims. 'What for?'

'Because,' Timmy says, 'my sister says whenever she gets a prick in her hand, she always puts it in cider.'

## Sweet nothings

Settling down at the bar to enjoy his drink, a man suddenly hears a voice say, 'You've got lovely ears, you have. Really lovely.'

He looks around, but doesn't see anybody, so he carries on with his drink.

A few seconds later, he hears the same voice saying, 'I really like your haircut, it really suits you.' Again, he looks round, and again he sees nothing.

He goes back to his pint, but as soon as it reaches his lips he hears the same voice. 'What a beautiful smile, it makes you look stunning.'

This time the man beckons the barman over. 'Did you hear that voice telling me how nice I looked?' he asks.

'Oh, think nothing of it,' says the barman. 'That's the peanuts on the bar – they're complimentary.'

## If you want to know the time ...

The police are ordered to clean up the high street for a big parade, and are patrolling the pavements when a drunk staggers towards them.

'Excuse me, offisher,' he says to one constable. 'Could you pleash tell me the time?'

The constable frowns at him. 'One o'clock,' he replies – before whacking the drunk over the head with his baton.

'Christ,' said the drunk, reeling. 'I'm glad I didn't ask you an hour ago.'

## Her indoors

Frank is enjoying a pint in the pub one afternoon with a friend.

'My wife will be on the plane now,' he says with a wistful smile.

'Really,' his friend says. 'Where's she off to, then?'

'Oh, nowhere,' says Frank. 'I've left her at home taking a couple of inches off the kitchen door.'

## Odds against

After her business goes bust, a blonde woman named Sharon finds herself in dire financial trouble – so desperate, in fact, that she resorts to praying.

'God, please help me,' she wails. 'I've lost my business, and if I don't get some money, I'm going to lose my car as well. Please let me win the lottery.'

Saturday night comes, and Sharon watches aghast as someone else wins it. Again, she begins to pray: 'God, please let me win the lottery! I've lost my business, my car, and I'm going to lose my house as well.'

Next Saturday night comes, and Sharon still has no luck. Once again, she prays. 'God, why haven't you helped me?' she cries, angrily. 'I've lost my business, my house, my car and now my children are starving. I've always been a good servant to you – PLEASE let me win the lottery just this once, so I can get my life back in order.'

Suddenly, there is a blinding flash of light as the heavens open above, and Sharon is confronted with the glowing, ethereal vision of God Himself.

'Sharon,' he booms. 'Meet me halfway on this. Buy a ticket.'

## What a prick

An extremely drunk man looking for a whorehouse stumbles into a chiropodist's office instead. Laboriously, he weaves over to the receptionist. Without looking up, she waves him over to the examination bed.

'Stick it through that curtain,' she says.

Looking forward to something kinky, the drunk pulls out his penis and sticks it through the crack in the curtains.

'That's not a foot!' screams the receptionist.

'Christ!' replies the drunk. 'I didn't know you had a minimum.'

## Two for the price of one

'I'm telling you, I've never been happier,' Carol tells her friend, 'I've got two boyfriends. One is just fabulous – handsome, sensitive, caring, considerate and he's got a fantastic sense of humour.'

'Well what on earth do you need the second one for?' asks her envious friend.

'Oh,' Carol replies, 'the second one is straight.'

## Past her prime

A self-obsessed bodybuilder is admiring his physique in the mirror one morning, and complimenting himself on his Herculean frame. Even his suntan is almost perfect, he notes – except, he realizes to his horror, for his groin, which is a pale, alabaster white. Annoyed, he decides to go to the beach and correct the situation. Arriving on an apparently deserted part of the shore, he undresses completely and buries himself in the sand – leaving only his knob above ground to catch the sun's rays.

However, before long, two old women come strolling along and notice his member waving in the sea breeze. After prodding it with her cane, one of the pensioners tuts. 'There is just no justice in the world,' she says.

The other old lady looks at her. 'What do you mean by that?' she says.

The first woman frowns. 'I'm 80 years old, and I've been chasing these things all my life,' she says. 'Now the damn things are growing wild and I'm too old to squat.'

# Never lie to kids

Little Johnny's mother is taking a bath, having recently been discharged from hospital where she had all of her pubic hair removed. Johnny comes into the bathroom as she's drying off, and asks her what happened to the hair.

'I've lost my sponge,' she says, and sends Johnny out to play.

A few moments later, Johnny reappears and tells his mother he thinks he's found her sponge.

'Oh, really,' his mum asks. 'Where is it?'

Johnny answers, 'The lady next door is washing daddy's face with it.'

# Flies never lie

While driving a truckload of manure, an old farmer is stopped by a policeman.

'You were speeding,' says the cop. 'I'm going to have to give you a ticket.'

'If you must,' the farmer says, watching the cop shoo away several flies.

'These flies sure are terrible,' the cop complains, swatting irritably.

'Yep,' the farmer says. 'Them are circle flies. They call them that because they circle a horse's tail.'

The cop looks at him angrily. 'You wouldn't be calling me a horse's ass now, would you?' he barks.

'Nope, I'm not,' replies the farmer. 'But you just can't fool them flies.'

# Always read the instructions

Three new inmates are sitting in their cell, contemplating their futures.

The first one takes out a mouth organ. 'At least I can keep myself amused by playing a little music. It'll help to pass the time.'

The second takes out a pack of cards. 'We can while away the time playing poker,' he says.

The third man takes out a box of tampons. 'What the hell are you going to do with those?' the other two ask.

He grins and says, 'It says on the box I can ride, swim, ski and play tennis with these.'

# Who can blame her?

What's the difference between a penis and a bonus?

Your wife will always blow your bonus.

## Smooth operator

The local paper in Leeds carries an advert for the job of 'fanny shaver'. A young hopeful rings up the number shown, and the man answers the phone asks him some questions. 'First things first,' he says. 'Are you single?'

'Oh yes,' says the applicant.

'That's good,' says the man, 'we've had a lot of trouble in the past with people who are married. Their wives get annoyed. Now, secondly, do you have a current ten-year passport?'

'Yes,' says the young applicant.

'Brilliant,' says the man. 'Often we find that people have a problem with travelling all over the globe. They seem to find the strain of jetting from LA to Milan to New York staying at top-class hotels a little bit too much to take.'

'Oh no, not me,' says the young hopeful. 'I love to travel.'

'Great,' says the man. 'And what about supermodels? Do you think you'd have a problem getting close to some of the most beautiful women in the world? You might even have to party with them and keep them company. How would you deal with that?'

'I'd be fine,' says the applicant. 'I love talking to women and I don't think I'd be intimidated.'

'Excellent,' says the man. 'Now, what about the shaving of the fanny? Would you get flustered peeling bikini bottoms off beautiful women, foaming them up and shaving their pubic regions? This sort of intimacy can often make a man all fingers and thumbs, you know.'

'No way,' says the young man. 'I have no problem with nudity or intimacy with gorgeous women. I'd be both discreet and charming.'

'Well,' says the man, 'you sound as if you could be just right for the job. I'll post you a coach ticket to Croydon.'

'Is that where my first job is?' asks the applicant.

'Oh no,' says the man. 'That's where the queue for the interviews starts.'

### Killing me slowly

What goes clip-clop, clip-clop, BANG! Clippetty-clop, clippetty-clop?
An Amish drive-by shooting.

## Overheard ... in Los Angeles

**AMW:** Vaguely bimboid woman on the fringes of the entertainment industry ('Actress, Model, Whatever ...')

**Boulevard boys:** Men whose income derives from the provision of sexual favours on Santa Monica Boulevard.

**Gas queens:** Customers of the above.

**Fruit-and-nut run:** The unofficial code name used by pilots for the flight to LA.

**Gated community:** Estate agent gabble for an area surrounded by razor wire and security cameras.

**Glassphalt:** Stardust, or tiny speckle of glass, set in the pavement of Hollywood Boulevard.

**Prone-out:** To take a close look at the road, when asked to lie face down by a member of the constabulary.

**TV parking:** The once-in-a-lifetime experience of finding a parking space right in front of where you want to be, like on television.

## Sorted!

One fine day in the forest, Mr Rabbit is on his daily run. when he sees a giraffe rolling a joint.

'Giraffe, oh Giraffe!' he calls. 'Why do you do drugs? Come run with me instead!' So the giraffe stops rolling his joint and runs with the rabbit.

Then they come across an elephant doing lines. 'Elephant, oh Mr Elephant, Why do you do drugs? Come run with us instead.' So the elephant stops snorting, and goes running with the other two animals.

Then they spy a lion preparing a syringe. 'Lion, oh Mr Lion' cries the rabbit, 'Why do you do drugs? Come run with us instead.'

But no – with a mighty roar, the lion smashes the rabbit to smithereens.

'No!' cry the giraffe and the elephant. 'Why did you do that? All he was trying to do was to help you out!'

The lion growls at them. 'That fucking rabbit always makes me run around the forest when he's whizzing his tits off.'

# Anal intruder

One day a man has a terrible stomach complaint and goes along to his doctor to see what can be done about it. The doctor tells him that he is very ill, but that he can cure his condition with a course of suppositories, inserted deep into his arse every six hours.

'Right,' says the doctor, 'bend over and I'll do the first one for you.' The man bends down and the doctor sticks the suppository deep into his hole. He then gives the man his course and sends him home.

At home six hours later the man realizes that he can't stick the suppository far enough up his arse on his own, and he asks his wife to help him insert the slippery bullet. After explaining to her what to do the man bends over. His wife puts one hand on her husband's shoulder to brace herself and thrusts the suppository really hard into his arse. To her horror, the man lets out a desperate, blood-curdling scream.

'My God!' she cries. 'What's the matter? Have I hurt you?'

'No,' replies the man. 'But I've just realized that when the doctor did it he had both hands on my shoulders.'

# Brawn, not brains

After hours of drinking heavily, Bob is sitting in a bar when, through his bloodshot eyes, he notices a figure sitting next to him. Feeling very jovial, the bloke turns to the blurry figure and says: 'Do you want to hear a blonde joke?'

The figure next to him snorts. 'Listen, mate,' comes a female voice, 'I weigh 175 lbs and am the British Women's kick-boxing champion. I am also blonde. My blonde friend next to me weighs 190 lb and is the Women's European arm-wrestling champion. Finally, my other friend at the end of the bar weighs 235 lb and is the Women's World power-lifting champion. She, too, is a natural blonde. Now, do you still want to tell that blonde joke?'

The guy pondered this for a while.

'Hmmm,' he replied finally. 'Not if I have to explain it three times.'

# Feeding time

What do elephants have for dinner?

An hour – just like the rest of the animals.

# Don't get lost in the woods

After graduating from the University of Arkansas, a young journalist gets a job at a tiny provincial newspaper in the middle of the prairies. His first assignment is to write a human-interest story, so he goes out to the country to do his research. Driving through the cornfields, he spies an old farmhand and introduces himself.

'I was just wondering, sir' the young hack asked. 'Out here in the middle of nowhere – has anything ever happened that made you happy?'

The old-timer furrowed his weathered brow for a moment.

'Yep!' he exclaimed, suddenly. 'One time my neighbour's daughter, a good-looking girl, got lost. So we formed a posse, and went out and found her. After we all screwed her, we took her back home.'

The young journo blanched. 'I can't print that!' he cried. 'Can't you think of anything else that happened that made you happy?'

The farmer thought again. 'Yeah!' he said, finally. 'One time one of my neighbour's sheep got lost. After forming a posse, we found it and all screwed it before we took it back home.'

'Christ!' says the young man. 'I can't print that either!' He thinks for a while. 'Okay – has anything ever happened around here that made you sad?'

The old man looked at the ground. 'Well,' he said sheepishly. 'I got lost once.'

## Memory lapse

A young man walks out of a newsagent's and spies an old man on a park bench crying his eyes out. So the youth goes over to the howling pensioner to see if he's all right. 'Are you okay?' he asks.

'No, it's my birthday today, I'm 82', blubs the old man.

'Eighty-two! But you look great for your age, you should be happy', continues the young man.

'Yeah, and I got married yesterday too – to a 25-year-old blonde bombshell', explains the old man.

The sympathetic young man thinks he's sussed the old man's misery and continues his line of enquiry, 'And you're too old to fulfil your conjugal responsibilities, I suppose?'

'No, not all, we enjoy a full and loving sexual relationship and get down to it five times a day. That's not the problem at all', says the old man, who is still crying.

'Look, mate, I'm 25 and even I don't enjoy that much sex, you lucky sod', says the dumbfounded lad. 'So why are you crying?'

The old man looks up and says wistfully, 'I've forgotten where I live'.

## What a dump!

A drunk staggers down the main street of a town and up the church steps. He manages to open the church door and falls into the silent building. On his hands and knees he weeps as he struggles to pull himself to his feet, half crawling and half walking towards the front of the church. He crashes from pew to pew softly crying, 'Oh God help me, God help me', until he finally makes it into the confessional box.

Having observed the man's sorry progress the priest sits silently in the booth, waiting to hear the drunk's tale. He waits for several minutes, hearing the drunk moan and groan, until finally there is a lengthy silence from the drunk's side of the confessional. At last the priest speaks.

'May I help you my son?' he says.

'I don't know father', the drunk replies. 'It depends on whether or not you have any paper on your side'.

## Take matters into your own hands

Plucking up the courage, a young man goes to a massage parlour for the first time. As he's not sure when to ask for the dirty deed, he lies on the leather bed, frustratedly getting more and more aroused. After a few minutes, the masseuse notices his growing erection. 'Perhaps sir would like a wank?' she breathes. The man gulps. 'Yes please,' he stutters.

With that, the lady leaves the room, and returns a full 20 minutes later. 'Well,' she says, popping her head round the door. 'Finished?'

## Overheard ... in the SAS

**Basha:** A hole in the ground, a thing made of branches — basically, your house in a war.

**Bone:** Naff, stupid, not a good thing to be.

**Cuds:** Utterly charming, cow-sick name for the countryside.

**Eppie scoppie:** To throw a wobbler.

**Head shed:** Anywhere the bosses congregate.

**Jundie:** A poor unfortunate Iraqi soldier.

**On my chinstrap:** A bit on the weary side.

**REMF:** A loser (comes from Rear Echelon Mother-Fucker).

**RTU'd:** Returned To Unit — a polite way of saying someone has been sacked.

**Ruperts:** Not entirely complementary reference to the officers, and their suspiciously upper-class demeanour.

**Scaley:** Bizarre, reptilian nickname for a signaller.

**Slime:** Repulsive, vicious handle for an intelligence officer.

**Slot:** To kill someone.

**Tab:** Not something to smoke in the barracks, but a nice, long, health-giving march.

## Undercover story

What's pink and hangs out your pants?
Your mum.

## Load of balls

A man enters a barbershop for a shave. While the barber is foaming him up, he mentions the problems he has getting a close shave around the cheeks. 'I have just the thing,' says the barber – and takes two small wooden balls from a nearby drawer. 'Just place these between your cheek and gum.' The client places the ball in his mouth and the barber proceeds with the closest shave the man has ever experienced. After a few strokes the client is very impressed.

'Just one thing,' he asks in a garbled voice. 'What if I swallow them?'

'No problem,' says the barber. 'Just bring them back tomorrow like everyone else does.'

## Thinking ahead

A man walks into a bar and sees a beautiful woman sitting on her own. Thinking quickly he buys a drink and goes over to sit next to her.

'Hello,' he says, 'Can I show you something?'

The woman looks him up and down. 'Okay,' she says, 'What is it you want to show me?'

The man rolls up his sleeve and points to his watch.

'You see this watch?' he says. 'It enables me to tell anything about the person I am talking to without asking them a single question.'

'Rubbish,' the woman replies, 'Your watch can't tell you anything about me.'

'Right,' the man says, and he stares intently at the watch for a few seconds, 'I can tell you haven't got any knickers on.'

'Sorry,' the woman replies, 'But your watch must be broken. I've got knickers on.'

The man looks at his watch in confusion, then gradually a smile of recognition spreads across his face.

'Oh, that's right,' he says, 'I set it ten minutes fast this morning.'

## www.oj.com

Where would you find OJ Simpson's website on the Internet?
Slash, slash, backslash, escape.

# A fishy story

A beautiful young lady wearing a lovely summer dress is sitting peacefully in a railway carriage on her own when a crusty traveller enters the compartment, eating a tray of king prawns. The filthy youth sits down opposite the woman, shelling his prawns and flicking the debris onto the floor, occasionally tossing one onto the young lady's lap with a sneer. When he's finished his meal he casually screws up the carton he's been eating out of and throws it at the girl's face.

The young lady then calmly stands up, picks up the shells from the floor, put them in the carton and throws the whole sorry mess out of the window. She then walks over to the communication cord and pulls it.

'You silly bitch', the crusty says with a sneer, 'That'll cost you a £50 fine.'

'Yes', the young lady replies, 'And when the police smell your fingers it'll cost you ten years.'

# Last requests

Three criminals are in hell waiting to be punished for their sins, and the Devil says, 'Before I plunge you into the fiery abyss, you can have one cool beer as a last privilege.'

The first criminal in the line-up is Jeffrey Dahmer.

'What drink do you want?' asks Satan.

'I would love a Budweiser', replies Dahmer, and sure enough he's given a can of it before being tossed into agony.

The Devil repeats his question to the second criminal.

'I would like some Foster's', says Ronnie Kray, and he gets some of the amber nectar before his punishment.

Finally, the Devil asks the third man, Fred West, what beer he'd like before being burnt for eternity.

'Oh, that's easy', says Fred. 'I could murder some Tennent's.'

# The generous judge

'Mr Quinn, I have reviewed your case very carefully', the divorce court judge said, 'And I have decided to award your wife a sum of £500 a month.'

'That seems more than fair, your Honour', said Mr Quinn. 'And I shall do my best to send her and the kid a few quid each month myself.'

## Not reading the signs

There once was a mobster who employed a deaf and dumb accountant. For years all went well between the two, until one day the mobster decided to doublecheck his books and found that he was short by $10 million. Enraged, he sent for the accountant, who returned accompanied by his brother, who could speak sign language.

'Tell your bastard brother I want to know where my $10 million's gone,' the furious gangster swore at the brother.

After a quick exchange the translating brother reported that the accountant knew nothing about the missing millions.

The angry Mafioso then pulled out a gun and held it to his accountant's head. 'You tell this lying son of a whore that if he don't tell me where my money is in the next 20 seconds, I'll blow his fucking brains out.'

The brother duly translated this message, and the accountant furiously signalled back that the money was hidden under a bed in his house.

'Well,' growled the thug, 'What did the little rat say?'

'He said,' replied the brother, 'that you haven't got the balls to do it.'

## In hot water

Nervously pacing up and down a hospital corridor, a man waits as his wife gives birth to their first child. After a long labour the doctor comes out and tells the man that he is the father of a baby boy. The man is overjoyed, and rushes in to his wife who smiles weakly and gives him the child.

Overcome, the tearful father asks the midwife if there is anything he can do to help. Sensing that the dad wants to share in the occasion, the midwife tells him to take the baby and bathe it next door.

After a few minutes the midwife pops in to see how the man is getting on – then jumps back in dismay when she sees what the new dad is doing. He has two fingers firmly lodged up the infant's nose and is dragging the child through the water in figure of eights.

'Good God!' she shouts. 'That's not how to bathe a newborn!'

'It bloody well is,' the man replies, 'when the water's this hot.'

## The aerial wedding

Two TV aerials meet on a rooftop, fall in love and decide to get married. On the big day the ceremony was awful, but the reception was excellent.

## Calm down! Calm down!

At the end of a tiny deserted bar is a huge Scouse bloke – 6 feet 5 inches tall and 350 lbs. He's having a few beers when a short, well-dressed and obviously gay man walks in and sits beside him. After three or four beers, the queer finally plucks up the courage to say something to the big Liverpudlian.

Leaning over, he cups his huge ear: 'Do you want a blow job?' he whispers. At this, the massive Merseysider leaps up with fire in his eyes and smacks the man in the face. Knocking him off the stool, he proceeds to beat him all the way out of the bar. Finally, he leaves him, badly bruised, in the car park and returns to his seat as if nothing has happened.

Amazed, the bartender quickly brings over another beer. 'I've never seen you react like that,' he says. 'Just what did he say to you?'

'I'm not sure,' the big Scouser replies. 'Something about a job.'

## Courting controversy

Following a hard day in court, a judge decides to go to the pub. Nine pints and seven whiskies later, he staggers out of the boozer and starts to walk home. Unfortunately, on his way he feels sick and he throws up all over his suit. Arriving home, he uses his fine legal mind to explain the mess to his wife. 'Some filthy tramp vomited all over me,' he moans, and his sympathetic wife makes him a nice cup of tea.

The next day the judge comes home and decides to make his story more convincing. 'You'll never guess what?' he says to his wife, 'The tramp that threw up on me was in court today. I gave him six months!'

'Well,' she replies, 'You should have given him a year, because he shat in your pants as well.'

## Overheard ... at Heathrow

**Blast:** Inhospitable burst of air from a jet engine that sprays high-velocity stones at the ground staff.

**Clean news:** Fresh newspapers for a plane.

**Crossing live:** Driving across a runway in use.

**Dirty and nude:** Slum-like state of planes before restocking and extensive hoovering.

**Eccies:** Low-lifes, also known as economy class passengers.

**Kosher dwell-time:** Lengthy post-check-in wait experienced by El Al passengers.

**Peaky:** A terminal that is only busy in surges.

**Root route:** Long-haul flight on which passengers regularly take the opportunity to make love beneath a courtesy blanket.

**Terminal zero:** The royal suite, probably queue free most of the time.

**Tortoise:** Amphibious rescue machine designed to cope with crashes into the Perry Oaks sewage lagoons.

**Weepers and wailers:** Damp-hankied types waving loved ones skywards.

# Fit for duty?

During a shortage of eligible men, a bear, a pig and a rabbit are called up for national service. While waiting for the medical examinations, they all admit they're terrified of being killed.

'I'm ungainly and pink,' says the pig, truthfully. 'The enemy will see me a mile off – so I decided to chop my tail off.'

The rabbit nods sagely – and the bear realizes the bunny's ears have been removed. 'I just hope it works,' says the rabbit.

Mystified, the bear watches as both animals enter the examination room – then return, smiling.

'We're free to go,' says the rabbit. 'They said a rabbit without ears is not a proper rabbit, and a pig without a curly tail is not a proper pig!'

He's about to leave with the pig when the bear pipes up.

'Hang on a minute!' he cries. 'I'm massive and slow – I'd not last a day.'

The other two look at the bear. 'Well,' says the rabbit, 'Your sharp teeth could be useful in combat. You might want them removed ...'

Nodding miserably, the bear lies down – and the other animals start kicking his fangs out. Eventually the dazed bear, blood pouring from his mouth, stumbles through the door. A moment later he returns.

'Did you get let off?' says the pig.

'Yesh,' splutters the bear. 'Apparently I'm too fat.'

# Hard to believe

A elderly gentleman shuffles into a drug store and asks for Viagra.

'That's no problem,' says the pharmacist. 'How many do you want?'

'Just a few, maybe four,' says the pensioner. 'But could you cut them into four pieces?'

'That won't do you much good,' replies the pharmacist.

The customer looks at him and sighs.

'I'm 83 years old – I'm not interested in sex anymore,' he says. 'I just want it to stick out far enough so I don't piss on my shoes.'

# Beer goggles

What is the difference between a dog and a fox?

About eight pints.

## Can't see the woods for the tree

A traffic policeman pulls a car over on a lonely back road and approaches the lady driver. 'Ma'am, why were you weaving all over the road?' he asks.

'Oh, officer!' the woman replies. 'Thank goodness you're here! I almost had a terrible accident. Swerving to avoid a tree, I looked up to find another tree right in front of me. So I pulled the car over to the right and there, yet again, was another tree in front of me!'

The copper nods, then points to the rear-view mirror.

'Ma'am,' he says, patiently. 'That's your air freshener.'

## Is it malignant?

A man walks into a bar with a big green bullfrog on his head.

'Where did you get that?' the barman asks.

'Would you believe,' the bullfrog replies, 'it started out as a tiny little wart on my arse?'

## The missing pen

A doctor is sitting in his surgery preparing to write out a prescription for a patient. He reaches into the top pocket of his white coat and pulls out a rectal thermometer.

'Damn!' he swears. 'That means some arsehole must have my pen.'

## Never satisfied

A Jewish grandmother is watching her grandchild playing on the beach – when a huge wave washes over him, pulling him out to sea. Falling down on her knees in the sand, the grandma begins to pray:

'Please God, save my only grandson! He is my life and the future of our family! With all my years of faith, please return him to us safely!'

Just then a huge wave rolls back onto the beach, bringing the bewildered lad back onto the sand, good as new.

The grandma looks up to the sky. 'He had a hat,' she bellows.

# Hidden love

An elderly Frenchman went to his parish priest, and asked to confess.

'Of course, my son', said the priest.

'Well, Father, at the beginning of World War Two, a beautiful woman knocked on my door and asked to hide from the Germans. I concealed her in my attic, and they never found her.'

'That's a wonderful thing, my son, and nothing that you need to confess,' said the priest.

'It's worse, Father. I was weak, and told her that she had to pay for rent of the attic with her sexual favours,' continued the old man.

'Well, it was a very difficult time, and you took a large risk – you would have suffered terribly at their hands if the Germans had found you hiding her.'

The man nodded solemnly, as the padre went on. 'I know that God will balance the good and the evil. He will judge you kindly,' the priest concluded.

'Thanks, Father', said the old man. 'That's a load off of my mind. Can I ask another question?'

'Of course, my son', said the priest.

'Do I need to tell her that the war is over?'

# Role reversal

A female journalist goes out to Kuwait to do a story on gender roles, just
before the outbreak of the Gulf War in 1991. She notes with some dismay
that the women of the country customarily walk about 10 feet behind their
men. Several years later the same journalist returns to the country to see
if there has been any change in these gender roles. She is surprised to find,
on her return, that the men now walk ten feet behind their women. Amazed
at this, she approaches a young lady.

'This is marvellous,' she says. 'What enabled the women here to effect such
a reversal of roles?'

'Simple,' the young woman replies. 'Land mines.'

# Lateral thinking

Three men reach the final round of tests to join the SAS, and are called
together to speak with the interviewer.

'Do you love your wife?' says the officer.

'Sir, yes I do, sir,' say the recruits in unison.

'And do you love your country?'

'Sir, yes sir,' say the men.

'But what do you love more, your wife or your country?'

The recruits do not hesitate: 'Sir, my country, sir.'

The interviewer stares at them: 'We want you to prove this. Your wives are
sitting in separate rooms nearby – take this gun and go and kill your loved one.'

The first man gulps and stares at the gun for a few minutes.

'I can't do it,' he says, and leaves.

Turning white, the second man goes into the room, and all is silent for about
five minutes. Soon the door opens and the man, sweaty with his tie loosened,
puts down the unfired gun and leaves.

The final interviewee looks long and hard and the revolver, then slowly
paces into the adjoining room. After a brief silence, the interviewer hears
the sound of a gunshot. There's a brief pause, then an almighty crashing
sound and a woman's scream.

Grinning and breathless, the final recruit emerges from the room and puts
the gun on the table. The interviewer looks up at him and says 'What the
hell happened?'

'The gun you gave me was filled with blanks,' says the man, breathing heavily.
'So I had to beat her to death with the chair.'

# A man's best friend

Leaving a cafe with his morning cup of coffee, a man notices a most unusual funeral procession approaching the nearby cemetery. Moving up the street slowly is a black hearse, followed closely behind by a second black hearse. Behind this, with head bowed, walks a solitary man walking a pit bull on a leash. Behind him are about 200 men walking single file.

Curiosity getting the better of him, the man respectfully approaches the man walking the dog.

'I know now is a bad time to disturb you,' he says to the mourner. 'But I've never seen a funeral like this. Who has passed away?'

The bereaved looks up. 'Well, that first hearse is for my wife.'

'What happened to her?' the first man asks.

The funeral-goer looks down at his pit bull. 'My dog attacked and killed her.' The man nods solemnly 'Well, who is in the second hearse?'

'My mother-in-law,' the man answers. 'She was trying to help my wife when the dog turned on her.'

A poignant and thoughtful moment of silence passes between the two men.

'Could I borrow that dog?' says the first man, finally.

The mourner looks at him wearily. 'Get in line.'

# That's the spirit

A landlord is shining glasses behind the bar when in walks a businessman.

'What'll you have?' asks the publican.

'A scotch, please,' replies the businessman.

The bartender hands him the drink, and says 'That'll be two quid.'

'What are you talking about?' says the man, angry. 'I don't owe you anything for this.'

# The ugly bug ball

After a heavy night, a man rolls over to find possibly the ugliest woman in the world sleeping peacefully beside him. Aghast, he very gently slides his arm out from under her, gets up, and dresses as fast as he can. Stopping only to leave a £20 note on the bureau, he tip-toes out – only to feel a tug on his trouser leg. Looking down, he sees a girl just as ugly as the one in the bed.

'What?' she smiles, toothlessly. 'Nothing for the bridesmaid?'

## The lazy sons

Ron and Reg are sitting in the café moaning about the younger generation.
'My son must be the laziest little bastard in Britain,' Ron says, sipping his tea.
'You've got no chance, mate,' Reg answers. 'My boy Gary is the laziest little
shit I've ever seen.'

The two men continue to argue and decide to visit each other's houses to
witness the lazy lads first hand. First they go to Ron's house, where his son
is lying on the sofa watching *This Morning*.

'Nip up the road and get me 20 Marlboro will you?' Ron asks his lad.
'Get them yourself,' the boy says. 'I'm watching television.'
'Go on, son,' Ron says. 'I'll give you a tenner if you just go and get me
some fags.'
'Bollocks,' the boy says. 'I'm not shifting.'

Ron and Reg then head over to Reg's house. They walk into the living room
where the curtains are shut and the telly is blaring out *Oprah*. Jimmy, Reg's
son, is sitting in front of the fire, the room is unbearably hot and the boy is
weeping softly. The two men stare at the boy in disbelief: an 18-year-old lad
sitting at home openly crying over a television show. Jimmy doesn't even look
up as the two men come into the room, he just sits in his chair, staring at the
television screen, crying like a baby.

Annoyed at his son's apathy, Reg finally walks over and turns off the
television. But it doesn't do any good and Jimmy just carries on weeping,
staring into space.

'What's the matter, son?' Reg asks.
'I'm burning,' Jimmy replies.

## It's a small world

A Czechoslovakian man feels his eyesight is getting worse, and visits an
optician. He sits down in the chair, and the optician points at the bottom line
of the eye-test: CZYFHRGRV.

'Can you read this?' asks the doctor.
'Read it?' says the Czech. 'Doc, I know the guy!'

## Watching your figure

A nought and a figure of eight are walking through the desert, when the
nought turns the eight and says, 'Why have you got that belt pulled so tight?'

# Skilled worker

A dog walks into the Job Centre and asks the man at the counter if they have any vacancies. The man is stunned. 'You're a talking dog!' he cries. 'What a wonderful talent you have. I'm sure we can find work for you no problem.'

At this the dog becomes agitated. 'Look,' he says. 'Don't mess me about. Have you got any jobs or not?'

'Okay,' says the man. 'Just sit tight. I'll make a call and I'll have you working in no time.'

With that the man phones Billy Smart's Circus. 'I've got a talking dog here,' the man says to Billy. 'Can I send him down to you?'

Billy is ecstatic. 'All my life I've been looking for a talking dog,' he says. 'You get him down here tomorrow morning and he can name his wage.'

The dog's still wary. 'What will I be doing for Mr Smart?' he asks.

The man is puzzled. 'I imagine you'll be the Talking Dog in the circus,' he says.

'Oh, that's no good to me, mate,' the dog says. 'I'm a plumber.'

## The cowpoke

Three cowboys were sitting around a campfire, out on the lonesome trail, each with a tale of bravado for which cowboys are famous.

'I must be the meanest, toughest cowboy there is,' the first cowboy said with a drawl. 'Why, just the other day, a bull got loose in the corral and gored six grown men before I wrestled it to the ground, by the horns, with my bare hands.'

The second cowboy couldn't stand to be bested. 'Why, that's nothing,' he said. 'I was walking down the trail yesterday when a 15 feet rattler made a move for me. I grabbed it with my bare hands, bit its head off and sucked down all of its poison. And I'm still here to tell the tale.'

All this time, the third cowboy remained silent, and the first two turned to look at him as he slowly stoked the red-hot coals with his penis.

## Roadkill

A young brickie starts work on a farm, and the boss sends him out to the local supplier for more cement. As dusk falls, though, he's still not returned – so the boss calls him on the CB radio.

'I've got a problem, Boss,' comes the reply. 'I've hit a pig!'

The foreman sighs. 'Ah well, these things happen sometimes,' he says, sympathetically. 'Just drag the carcass off the road so nobody else hits it.'

'But he's not dead, boss,' says the young man. 'He's tangled up on the bull bar. I've tried to untangle him, but he's kicking and squealing in a horrible way. He's a real big mutha, boss – I'm afraid he's going to hurt me!'

'Never mind,' says the boss. 'There's a shotgun in the back of the truck. Get that and shoot him. Then drag the carcass off the road and come home.'

Another half an hour goes by, but there's still no word from the youngster. The boss gets back on the CB. 'What's the problem, son? Did you drag the pig off the road like I said?'

Through the radio crackle comes the reply: 'Yeah boss – but his motorbike is still jammed under the truck.'

## Eighteen hours to live

A woman comes home from the doctor and tells her husband she has only 18 hours to live.

'That's terrible!' cries her husband, 'What would you like to do during your last hours? I'll try to make it as memorable as possible for you.'

'Well,' she said, 'First, I want to take a long romantic walk, then have a quiet dinner at my favourite restaurant. But ultimately, I want to go to bed with you and make passionate love all night long.'

'Gee, honey,' says her husband, shaking his head 'I don't know about that "all night long" stuff. After all, I've got to get up in the morning.'

## Drunk driving (iv)

A man is driving home after drinking one too many following a round of golf. After pulling him over to the side of the road, a policeman informs him that he is too drunk to drive.

'Too drunk to drive?' the man says. 'Officer, I can barely putt!'

## It's a question of timing

Three old men are sitting around chatting about their respective toilet habits.

'The best thing that could happen to me,' says the 80 year-old, 'would just to be able to have a good pee. I stand there for 20 minutes, and it dribbles and hurts. I have to go over and over again.'

The 85-year-old nods in agreement. 'The best thing that could happen to me,' he laments, 'Is if I could have one good bowel movement. I take every kind of laxative I can get my hands on and it's still a problem.'

But the 90 year-old is shaking his head.

'That's not my problem,' he says. 'Every morning at 6:00am sharp, I have a good long slash. And then at 6:30am sharp I usually crimp off a length too.'

'So what's the problem?' chorus the others.

'Well,' says the pensioner, 'The best thing that could happen to me would be if I could wake up before 7:00am.'

## The spelling contest

A boy comes home from school looking sheepish. 'Dad,' he moans, 'We had a class spelling contest today, and I failed on the very first word.'

'Ah, that's okay, son,' says his father, looking over his glasses at him. 'What was the word?'

The son looks even more miserable. 'Posse,' he replies.

His father bursts out laughing.

'Well, no wonder you couldn't spell it,' he roars. 'You can't even pronounce it!'

## Under arrest

Did you hear Vanessa Feltz was held at by customs at Heathrow
– for smuggling drugs?
Allegedly, she had 40 lbs of crack in her knickers.

## Overheard ... at customs

**Bait:** Not maggots or breadcrumbs, but a shady-looking person who acts as a diversion for a big-time drugs courier.

**Blue:** A substance positively identified as cocaine.

**CES:** When you've been arrested, you want one of these. It's a Certified Empty Stomach.

**Elbowing:** Wearing a pricey watch up your sleeve to avoid paying the duty.

**Frost-box:** A special see-through toilet which lets the Customs men examine your stools as they drop.

**Pot special:** Flight BA262 from Kingston, Jamaica.

**Rummaging:** What sniffer dogs do to suspicious baggage.

**Queening:** A popular job with the righteous – it's burning seized drugs at the HM Warehouse.

**Stuffers:** Illegal drug importers who chose to transport tubes of drugs handily stored up their anus.

**X at Hill:** The X-ray check at Hillington Hospital near Heathrow for a gut full of swallowed condoms.

## Car trouble

A boy is walking down the road one day when a car pulls over. 'If you get in the car,' the driver says, 'I'll give you £10 and a packet of sweets.' The boy refuses and keeps on walking.

A little further up the road the man again pulls over. 'Okay,' he says. 'How about £20 and two packets of sweets?'

The boy tells the man to piss off and carries on walking.

Still further up the road the man again pulls to the curb.

'Right,' he says. 'This is my final offer – £50 and all the sweets you can eat.' The little boy stops walking, goes towards the car and leans in. 'Look,' he hisses. 'You bought the fucking Skoda, Dad, and you have to live with it.'

# Building site blunder

An Italian, an Irishman and a Chinese fellow are hired at a construction site. The foreman points out a huge pile of sand and says to the Italian guy, 'You're in charge of sweeping.'

He then turns to the Irishman. 'You're in charge of digging.'

Finally, he turns to the Chinaman. 'And you're in charge of supplies. Now, I have to leave for a little while. I expect you guys to make a dent in that pile.'

Two hours later, the foreman returns to find the pile of sand untouched, and the Italian and Irishman standing nearby looking sheepish.

'Why didn't you sweep any off it?' he asks the pair.

The Italian looks at him. 'We didn't have a broom or shovel. You said the Chinese guy was in charge of supplies, but he disappeared and I couldn't find him.'

Annoyed, the foreman storms off to find the errant Oriental. Just then, the Chinaman leaps out from behind the pile of sand.

'Supplies!' he yells.

# The future's Rosy

While on a day out in Blackpool a man decides to go and visit a fortune teller. He goes into the hut of Gypsy Rose Lee and sees a middle-aged lady sitting at a table staring into a crystal ball. He sits down and she begins to tell his fortune. A smile breaks out and she begins to laugh.

'You're going to come into great wealth,' she says. 'You'll marry a beautiful woman and have a long and happy life, full of laughter and great sex.'

At this the man stands up, draws back his arm and delivers an almighty haymaker at the fortune teller, catching her right in the middle of her face and breaking her nose. She falls to the floor, stunned by the punch. Bleeding from her nose, she asks the man why he lamped her.

'Oh,' he says, 'I always like to strike a happy medium.'

# Wishful thinking

An old woman goes into a sex shop and asks the assistant if she can have a look at an assortment of vibrators. Despite a wide range of colours, shapes and sizes, none of them appeal to the old lady. She looks up and says to the assistant, 'Can I have a look at that tartan one up there on the shelf?'

'No,' replies the shop assistant. 'That's my thermos flask.'

## Taking things too far

Taking his seat on a flight, a businessman is bemused to see a parrot in the next seat. The plane takes off and the man asks the stewardess for a coffee. As he does, the parrot screeches, 'Yeah, and get me a double whisky too, you ugly cow!'

The stewardess walks off to get the drinks, but on her return has forgotten the man's coffee. She apologizes, and as she turns to get the coffee the parrot again squawks, 'Yeah, and get me another whisky you slack-arsed tart!'

By now the stewardess is rattled, and she returns with the whisky, but again no coffee. The man, having observed the parrot's success, decides to try the rude approach. 'I've asked you for coffee twice!' he bellows, 'Now get your lazy butt back there and get me a cup of coffee.'

Moments later he and the parrot are dragged from their seats and thrown out of the emergency exit by two stewards. They plunge downwards for a few seconds, then the parrot looks at the man and squawks, 'For someone who can't fly, you sure are a ballsy prat!'

## The slowest takeaway in the world

One evening a husband and wife are sitting at home, waiting for dinner guests to arrive. After putting the casserole in the oven the wife turns and screams, 'I've forgotten the nibbles! We can't have a party without nibbles! Go down into the garden and fetch some snails. I'll boil them up and serve them with a little garlic butter and lemon.'

The husband sets off to the end of the garden with a bucket and starts hunting for the snails. No sooner has he started when a beautiful woman leans over the fence and casually asks him if he wants to pop over to her place for a quick drink. The husband thinks that a quick snifter before dinner can't hurt, so he climbs over the fence and goes in.

After downing a martini, the woman grabs the man and begins kissing him. One thing leads to another and soon the pair are hard at it in bed. So hard, in fact, that the husband falls asleep for a couple of hours. Waking up in a panic, he grabs all his clothes and his bucket of snails, jumps back over the fence and hurtles into his own kitchen where his wife has nodded off. He trips up as he enters through the door and spills his bucket of snails over the lino and wakes her.

'Where the hell have you been?' she screams. The husband looks up at his livid wife, looks down at the scattered snails on the floor and shouts, 'Come on lads, we're nearly there!'

## Bang! Hish! Bang! Hish!

Joe was visiting a friend's rubber factory one day. They entered the first room, to the loud sound of 'Bang! Hish! Bang! Hish!'

'What are you making here?' asked Joe.

'Teats for a baby's bottle,' replied the owner. 'The bang makes the teat and the hish puts the hole in the end.'

The next room, however, was filled with different sounds: 'Bang! Bang! Bang! Bang! Hish! Bang! Bang!'

'This is where we make condoms,' explained the owner.

'So why,' asked Joe, 'Do the machines go hish every now and then?'

'Well,' says the owner, 'We have to make sure there are enough babies for our teats.'

# Radical surgery

When Ralph first noticed that his penis was growing larger and staying erect longer, he was delighted – as was his wife. But after several weeks – when his spam javelin had grown to nearly 20 inches – Ralph became quite concerned, so he and his wife went to see a prominent urologist. After an initial examination, the physician explained to the couple that, though rare, Ralph's condition could be helped through corrective surgery.

'How long will Ralph be on crutches?' the wife asked anxiously.

'Crutches? Why would he need crutches?' responded the surprised doctor.

'Well,' said the wife coldly, 'You *are* planning to lengthen his legs, aren't you?'

# Drive in comfort

Prior to competing in the 2001 Open Championships, Tiger Woods is touring the links courses in Ireland and pulls into a petrol station in his huge Mercedes.

'Howdy,' he says to the attendant. 'Can you fill her up?'

But as he pulls out the keys, two wooden tees fall out of his pocket.

'Sweet Mary!' says the attendant. 'And what are they?'

Tiger looks down, and smiles.

'They're for putting my balls on while I'm driving.'

'Bejasus!' cries the attendant. 'Those fellas at Mercedes think of everything.'

# Home from home

A guy walks into a bar down in Alabama and orders a gin and tonic. Surprised, the bartender looks at him.

'Ain't you from around here, boy?' he sneers.

'I'm from Pennsylvania,' the guy replies.

The bartender frowns. 'What do you do there?'

'I'm a taxidermist,' comes the reply.

The bartender laughs incredulously. 'A taxidermist!' he cries. 'What the hell is a taxidermist?'

The guy looks at him. 'I mount dead animals.'

The bartender smiles and turns to the rest of the bar. 'It's okay, boys,' he shouts. 'He's one of us!'

## Eating disorder

Two men are sitting in the waiting room at a doctor's surgery. The first man is gingerly holding his shoulder with a look of severe pain on his face, while the second has baked beans in his hair, fried egg down the front of his shirt and two sausages sticking out of his front pockets. The two men weigh each other up for a few minutes, then the second man asks the first what happened to him.

'My cat got stuck up a tree,' the man says, gripping his arm. 'I went up after him and fell out. I think I've broken my shoulder.'

The second man nods in sympathy.

'What about you, then?' the first man asks. 'What's wrong with you?'

'Oh, it's nothing serious,' the second man replies. 'I'm just not eating properly.'

## Groin strain

George's girlfriend decided she wanted to please her man, so one day she went out and bought a pair of crotchless panties. That night she lay on the bed and waited for George to come home. When he got in he was greeted by the sight of his woman lying on the bed with her legs spread, wearing nothing but her new underwear.

'Hi Georgie,' she said in a throaty voice. 'You want some of this?'

'Jesus Christ, no!' George screams. 'Look what it's done to your knickers!'

## Overheard ... at the car dealers

**On the drip:** Nothing to do with a leaky exhaust, but a car available on hire purchase.

**A chop:** A straight part-exchange deal.

**Toe-dropper:** A dealer who has been sold a dodgy car and tries to sell it on.

**Cut and shut:** Two cars that have been illegally welded together.

**A Billy:** A customer (from Billy Bunter – punter). As in 'there's a Billy out front.'

**Lemon car:** A new car that constantly needs repairing.

**All bogged up:** A part-exchange car full of the previous owner's rubbish.

**Rent:** A valid tax disc. As in, 'Has it got rent on the screen?'

**Falling out of bed:** What a customer does when he changes his mind after agreeing to buy.

**Smoker:** A diesel engine.

**Getting stubble:** What happens to a car that rides roughly on its test drive.

**Jalopy:** An old wreck.

# It fell down the stairs ...

In a bid to encourage teamwork, representatives of the Navy, Army and
Metropolitan Police are invited to a cross-forces outward-bound competition.
With the scores even at the end of the weekend, the three groups are set one
final task: to troop into the woods and bring back a rabbit.

The Navy go in first: there's 15 minutes of quiet rustling, before a single shot
rings out. Before long, one naval officer emerges grinning from the undergrowth
– clutching a bunny shot neatly between the eyes.

Next up were the Army – who, it became obvious from the smoke and crackling,
were adopting a slash 'n' burn technique. After an afternoon, one of the
infantrymen emerged beaming – holding another rabbit, albeit slightly charred.

Finally, it was the turn of the Met – highly confident they could secure
victory. They descend into the foliage, and quickly there are the echoes of
gunfire. This continues for hours until – a full day later – the policeman walk
out, triumphantly holding up ... a slightly bloodied squirrel

'What the hell are you doing?' shouts the coordinator. 'You're supposed to
get a rabbit.'

In reply, one of the Met officers wordlessly holds up the battered rodent. 'Listen
to me,' it squeaks, wild-eyed. 'I'm a rabbit! For the love of God, I'm a rabbit!'

# Drunk driving (v)

A man and a woman leave a party in their car late one night. After a couple of miles a police car signals the man to pull over. The policeman walks up to the couple.

'Good evening, sir,' he says. 'Do you realize you were doing 60 mph in a 55 mph zone?'

'I'm afraid I didn't,' the man says. 'I must have put my foot down to keep up with the traffic. I'm terribly sorry.'

'He's lying, officer,' the man's wife suddenly shouts. 'He clearly told me he was going to thrash the car's arse off to get back in time for the football.'

The policeman nods his head. 'I also noticed you were weaving in and out of the traffic in a reckless manner,' he says.

'Yes, I was,' the man replies. 'An insect flew into my eye and I lost control for a moment. I'm very sorry. Next time I'll pull over.'

'He's such a liar,' the man's wife interrupts again. 'He was laughing like a madman and pretending to be James Hunt.'

At this point the man finally snaps.'For fuck's sake woman,' he bellows. 'Shut your blabbering mouth before I fill it!'

'Does he always speak to you like this?' the cop asks the wife.

'Oh no, officer,' the wife says. 'Only when he's had eight pints and a couple of bottles of wine.'

# The quick-thinking sentry

A private is alone on sentry duty when the phone rings in his box.

'Hello? Hello?' a voice shouts down the phone. 'Are there many vehicles in the officer's car park?'

The sentry steps out of his box and looks across the road, where a solitary Bentley is parked. He goes back to the box and answers the caller.

'Only that fat bastard General Jackson's car,' he says.

'Do you know who you're talking to?' booms the voice down the line. 'This is General Jackson!'

'Do you know who you're talking to?' the private replies, completely unflustered.

'No,' General Jackson answers.

'Well, fuck off then, fat arse,' the private replies.

## Slide rule

A woman is drying herself after a shower when she suddenly slips and lands spread-legged on the bathroom floor. After trying to stand, she's realizes she's landed so hard her crotch created a vacuum, sucking her to the floor. She calls out to her husband for help. He tries with all his strength to lift her but she won't budge. So he goes next door and gets his neighbour. Both pull like oxen but she just won't move. She's well and truly stuck to the floor. Suddenly the neighbour says, 'Why don't we just get a hammer and break the floor tiles around her and lift her up that way?'

'Great idea,' says the husband, 'but just let me rub her boobs a little to arouse her.'

'Why?' asks the confused neighbour.

'So we can slide her into the kitchen. The tiles are cheaper in there.'

## Now wash your hands ...

A very attractive young lady walks up to the bar and calls over the barman, a tall fellow with a thick, full beard. The woman leans over the bar in her low-cut dress and reaches out to touch the man.

'Are you the landlord?' she asks, gently stroking his lustrous beard and running her fingers through his hair.

'No,' gulps the barman, only just managing to pull his eyes away from her ample cleavage. 'I just work here.'

'Well,' says the forward young lady, caressing the barman's beard with both hands. 'Can I talk to him?'

'Er, no,' says the by now highly excited barman. 'He's not actually in tonight.'

'Well, when you see him,' the blond purrs, gently caressing the barman's face, 'tell him there's no toilet roll in the ladies.'

## The eager employee

A young executive was working late one night, trying to impress his new boss. He stepped out of the office for a minute to get some coffee, and saw his boss standing at the shredder with a piece of paper in his hand.

'Do you know how to work this damn thing?' his boss bellowed.

The young man ran over and took the paper out of his hand. 'Oh yes, sir,' he said. 'It's quite simple.' He then fed the piece of paper into the shredder.

'Thank you, son,' the boss said. 'A couple of copies will be fine.'

## Overheard ... in Ulster

**Ablach:** Prepare the Imperial Leather, for an ablach is a dirty sloven.

**Borgeegle:** A mistake that disastrously ruins a piece of work.

**Blibber:** To whine like an infant, not a million miles from 'blubber'.

**Currymushy:** A jostling, enthusiastic and jolly crowd of people.

**Cockaninny:** Girl with a high opinion of herself, could do with a two-peg reduction.

**Drookin:** A bit on the damp side. Absolutely soaking wet in fact.

**Drumadudgeon:** A man who is just two things: bone and idle.

**Feerdy:** A big fit lad.

**Handymagandy:** Useless bloke.

**Liggerty:** Lanky and rather hopeless.

**On the blatter:** Taking a drink or ten.

**Ratterbrash:** Common as muck.

**Stag's throb:** For reasons known only to creatures with antlers, it means 'not far'.

**Thraveless:** To be without thrave is also known as carelessness.

**Throoharleen:** The bloke who is always tripping over and banging his head and spilling his drink. At the same time.

# Drop 'em!

With his elderly wife, Bill the pensioner goes to the doctor for his annual physical. After testing him with the stethoscope, the physician turns to him. 'Well, Bill,' he says. 'You seem fine but I'm going to need a urine sample, a stool sample and a sperm sample.'

Hard of hearing, Bill turns look at his wife. 'What did he say?' he yells.

His wife bellows back: 'He said he needs your underwear.'

# Does it come with a candle?

A man runs into a fishmongers with a giant carp under his arm. 'Do you sell fishcakes?' he says to the shop owner.

'Of course we do,' comes the reply.

The customer breathes a sigh of relief. 'Thank God,' he says, gesturing to the fish. 'It's his birthday.'

## Second choice

One morning Martha walks down to the post office to cash in her pension. Standing in the queue she spies her good friend Wynn, whom she hasn't seen in a couple of months. After an initial chat, the pair meet outside for a good old chin-wag.

'Hello Martha', Wynn says. 'How have you been?'

'I've been fine', Martha answers. 'A bit of trouble with the hips but nothing major.'

'Oh good', Wynn says. 'And how's George?'

'He's okay', Martha says. 'The gout plays up now and then, but he gets by. How have you been?'

'Well', says Wynn, 'I've not been too good actually.'

'Oh dear', says Martha. 'What's happened?'

'Two months ago Albert was out in the garden picking his cabbages when I heard a terrible scream', Wynn says. 'It was a massive heart attack. He was dead before the ambulance got there.'

'Dear Lord!' Martha says. 'What on earth did you do?'

'What could I do?' Wynn says. 'I opened a tin of peas.'

## Spreading the news

An old man stumbles into the confessional.

'Father!' he shouts. 'I'm an 81-year-old man and last night I made love to two 19-year-old twins!'

'Well', the priest replies, 'are you married? Have you committed adultery?'

'No, Father', the old man says. 'My wife passed away several years ago.'

'Have you remarried, my son?' asks the priest.

'No, Father', the old guy replies.

'You're Catholic?' the priest asks.

'No', the aged Lothario replies. 'I don't believe in religion.'

'Well', says the priest, 'why on earth did you feel the need to come and tell me?'

'If you'd slept with two 19-year-old twins', the old git answers, 'wouldn't you be telling everyone?'

## Puss in Boots

A midget goes to the doctor's, complaining that her lady's area hurts like hell every time it rains. The doctor helps her onto the examination couch, and begins to examine her. After a while, he has to admit that he can't find anything wrong with her bearded clam at all.

'I tell you what', says the physician. 'Next time it rains, come into the surgery so I can give your lamb hangings the once over while you're in pain.'

The dwarf agrees, and two days later returns to the doctor's waiting room during a torrential downfall. As she's in absolute agony, the doctor agrees to see her right away, and lifts her onto the examination table for a closer look.

'Yes, I can see the problem now', he says, and reaches for the scalpel.

The pygmy woman is alarmed, but feels she's in the hands of a professional. Thirty seconds later, it's all over and she is lifted down from the table.

'How does that feel?' asks the doctor.

The gnomic girl wanders around the room for a while.

'There's no pain at all', she replies, smiling. 'Amazing – what did you do?'

'It was easy', says the physician. 'I just took an inch off the top of each wellie.'

## Miss Piggy

One day, a lonesome cowboy wanders into a saloon in a dusty hell-hole of
a town and heads straight to the bar for an ice-cold beer. He swigs back
his beer, then he asks the barman where he might find a little lady to take
the taste of the trail out of his mouth.

'Ain't no women for a hundred miles,' the barman says. 'But there's a barnyard
out back chock full of prime livestock. Feel free to go out and help yourself to
any of the animals.' Disgusted, the cowboy swears he would never stoop so
low as to have sex with another species.

However, the next night he is overcome with longing and loneliness, and he
creeps into the barnyard to take a little look-see. He spies a fine-looking
piglet and takes her back to his hotel room, where he gives the little porker a
bubble bath, grooms her real nice and ties a tiny pink ribbon behind her ears.
Then he tucks his new friend under his arm and takes her down to the bar
for a drink.

But as he walks through the swinging doors of the saloon, a deathly hush
falls over the crowd. Dozens of the townfolk are sitting around with their
animals, and the new cowboy can't work out why all the men are staring at
him with such obvious shock.

'What's the matter with you people?' he yells. 'You're all doing the same thing.'
At this a man at the back of the saloon stands up and says, in a solemn
voice, 'We sure are, mister, but you can bet your life we'd never do it with
the sheriff's gal.'

## Big mamas

Newly married, George and Tina retire to their honeymoon bedroom – and
breathlessly start undressing each other for the first time. As Tina's panties slide
off, George eyes nearly pop out.

'Ooh!' he cries, 'You've got a lovely big arse!'

Furious, Tina whacks across the face and pushes him out onto the balcony in
just his socks. He's standing there, freezing, when the bloke in the room next
to him is similarly pushed out.

'Shit – it's my wedding night,' says the man. 'And I've been thrown out for
saying my wife had really big tits.'

Just then a third naked man is also forcefully ejected onto the next balcony.
'I suppose you put your foot in it as well' said George.

'No,' says the new bloke, shaking his head. 'But I bloody well could have.'

# He's had his chip

Elderly and cancer-ridden, a man lay dying in his bed. In death's agony, he suddenly smelled the aroma of his favourite chocolate chip cookies wafting up the stairs. Gathering his remaining strength, he lifted himself out of bed and slowly made his way out of the bedroom. Bracing himself by leaning on the banister, he stumbled downstairs, his muscles screaming with the pain of the effort.

He finally reached he kitchen and breathing heavily, he leaned against the door-frame. Was he already in heaven? There, spread out upon newspapers on the table, were literally hundreds of his favourite chocolate chip cookies. Was it a divine gift? Or one final act of love from his devoted wife, making sure he left this world a happy man?

Mustering his strength, he threw himself toward the table, landing on his knees. His parched lips parted, imagining the wondrous taste of biscuit that would make his last hours tolerable. Shakingly, his withered hand snaked over to the plate at the edge of the table. But, suddenly, it was smacked with a spatula. 'Stay out of those,' said his wife. 'They're for the funeral.'

# Overheard ... in the City of London

**Jub:** Normally preceded by an expletive. Applied to someone in the habit of losing a load of other people's money.

**Pussy pelmet:** A young female booking clerk, employed principally as decoration.

**A Lombard:** A manager in charge of a large pension fund thought likely to lose it all.

**Ship and shag:** An investment which guarantees a fat profit for little effort.

**A lady:** Five million pounds.

**Catching the Intercity:** Getting a salary of £125,000 a year.

**A Wimbledon:** An investment of roughly ten units.

**The pelican:** Whoever's been left to pay for the (invariably large) lunch bill.

**A grand old Duke of York:** A pension fund whose value goes up and then rapidly down again.

**Droopies:** City of London prostitutes.

**A Sherpa:** Ten million Singaporean dollars (Ten-sing)

**Dead cat bounce:** A two-or-three-day rise in a market that is ultimately spiralling downwards.

## I want to break free

A man is involved in a terrible cycling accident, in which he breaks all of his limbs. Waking up in hospital several days later, his legs hoisted in the air and his arms encased in plaster, he finds the doctor looking at him from a chair next to his bed.

'Oh,' the doctor says, 'you're awake. How do you feel, my man?'

'Considering I've had such a terrible accident, I really don't feel too bad,' the injured man replies. 'In fact, I feel pretty darn good.'

But as he finishes saying this, he suddenly leans to his left. The doctor, realizing the man has no means of support, grabs him and props him upright. Later on a nurse comes by to check on him and asks him how he's getting on.

'As I said earlier,' the injured man says, 'when you consider what I've been through I actually feel super.' And again, he begins to fall to one side. The nurse jumps forward and sits him upright, then goes on her way.

The next day the man's wife comes in and asks her husband how he's feeling. 'As I've told everyone,' the man says, 'I feel fine. I just wish these buggers would let me fart in comfort!'

PFFFT

# Like a virgin

A young woman goes to see the doctor to ask his advice on a very sensitive matter. 'I'm getting married on Saturday,' the distraught young lady cries, 'and my husband is convinced I'm a virgin. What he doesn't know is that I lost my virginity years ago. Is there any way I can convince him I am still chaste?'

'Medically, no,' the doctor replies. 'But I do have a suggestion which may help. On your wedding night, when you're getting ready for bed, slide an elastic band around your thigh. When your husband enters you, simply twang the band with your fingers and tell your husband the sound is your hymen snapping.'

On the big day, the newlyweds go up to their honeymoon suite. The bride goes into the bathroom and slips the elastic band around her thigh. The couple then get down to some serious married sex. Just as her husband enters her, the bride snaps the band and moans with what she thinks is a mixture of ecstasy and pain.

'What the hell was that?' her husband cries.

'Oooh,' the woman moans. 'That must have been my virginity snapping, honey.'

'Well,' shouts her husband, 'snap it back again. It's caught round my bollocks.'

# Tough decision

An old woman is complaining to her equally ancient friend that she no longer has sex with her husband.

'He looks at me, with my tits like rooftiler's mailbags, and my saggy arse and old minge,' she moans, 'and he's completely turned off.'

Her 88-year-old friend looks at her with scorn and says, 'What you want to do is get down to Anne Summers and get yourself some sexy underwear. No red-blooded man can resist the sight of a woman in pingers and red satin bra.'

The following day the old lady goes down to the sex shop and buys herself a peephole bra and a pair of crotchless panties. That night she hides on top of her bedroom wardrobe, waits until her husband gets into bed, then, clad only in her new shagging gear, leaps from the wardrobe with a mighty banshee scream of 'Superfanny!'

She lands on top of her shocked husband who, after several seconds, says, 'I think I'll have the soup, if that's all right.'

# Lonely this Christmas ...

What weighs 8 lbs and won't be plucked next Christmas?
John Denver's guitar.

# Strict discipline

One day, while cleaning her young son's room, a mother finds a sado-masochist magazine on top of his wardrobe. Unsure of how to confront him, she keeps the magazine and shows it to her husband when he comes home from work. Slowly, he flicks through the pictures of leather-clad dominatrix and whips, before handing it back to his wife without a word.
'Come on,' she says, exasperated. 'What should we do about this?'
He looks back at her solemnly.
'Well,' he says. 'I don't think you should spank him.'

# No need to rush

Just after taking off, the captain of a jumbo makes his customary announcement to the passengers about the length of the journey, expected arrival time and so on. But after he's finished he forgets to turn off the microphone, turns to his co-pilot and says:
'Right, I'll finish off this sandwich, then I think I'll nip back and fuck that new red-headed stewardess.'
In horror, the stewie, who is at the rear of the plane, rushes down the aisle to prevent the captain's indiscretion going any further. An old lady grabs her arm as she goes past.
'Why be in such a rush, dear,' she says, 'He said he had to finish his sandwich first.'

# Cheap round

A man walks into a bar and orders ten pints of lager, with a further 12 vodka chasers. The barman then watches, amazed, as the bloke downs them one after the other. Recovering, the customer says, 'I shouldn't have done that with what I've got.'
'What have you got?' says the barman.
The bloke looks at him guiltily. 'Oh, about a quid.'

## Holy hotdog

What did the Buddhist say to the hotdog seller?
Make me one with everything.

# Overheard ... military pilots

**Bag season:** Cold or wet weather (usually in autumn), which requires
pilots to wear cumbersome anti-exposure suits.

**To be up on the governor:** When you're about to have a tantrum.
The governor is the device that keeps the engine from overheating.

**To buy the farm:** To die. Now coming in to general usage, the phrase
is believed to refer to US government pay-offs to farmers who'd had their crops
destroyed by a crashed plane. The compensation was considered so generous
that the dead pilot had effectively 'bought the farm'.

**Check for light leaks:** Go to sleep at the controls.

**Sinking your teeth in the floorboard:** When you set your
sights on another aircraft, but end up getting so close that it shoots
you down instead.

**To flathead:** To do stunts, fly low or otherwise endanger your
aircraft just for the hell of it.

**Hinge head:** Commanding officer. Comes from the belief that all
officers receive lobotomies on reaching senior rank. The hinge enables
the brain to be re-inserted later.

**Kick the tyres and light the fires:** Overlook the routine
inspection of the aircraft before take off when the pilots are in a hurry.

**A leapex:** A stupid and unnecessary drill procedure.

**The loud handle:** The lever that operates the ejector seat.

**Playmates:** Pilots of aircraft taking part in the same exercise as you.

**Plumbers:** Very bad pilots.

**A puke:** A pilot who flies a different kind of aircraft to you.

**Shoes:** Non-flying aviation personnel.

**A tax return:** A wrecked aircraft. So-called because the tax-payers
have to fork out for a new one.

**A tits machine:** A favourite aircraft now out of service.
As in: 'The B52 – now that was a real tits machine'.

**Vultures' row:** The visitors gallery at an air base.

## Almost cured

After years in a psychiatric institute, a patient seems finally well enough to be released – so undergoes a final examination by the chief psychiatrist.

'Tell me,' says the doctor, 'if we release you, what do you intend to do with your life?'

The inmate thinks for a moment. 'While I look forward to returning to my proper life, I would certainly avoid making the same mistakes. I was a nuclear physicist, and the stress of my work in weapons research lead to my breakdown. Consequently, in the future I shall confine myself to less stressful work in pure theory.'

'Marvellous,' says the shrink.

'Or else,' ruminated the inmate, 'I might teach, or write books – I could help educate the next generation of scientists.'

'Absolutely,' said the head. 'So many possibilities. But what if it doesn't work out?'

The patient grins. 'Oh, that's fine,' he says confidently. 'I can always fall back on the fact I'm a teapot.'

## Clever dick

A rich, lonely widow decides she needs a man in her life – so she places an advert in the local paper. It reads:

*Rich widow looking for kind man to share life and fortune with. Must never beat me up or run away – and has to be great in bed.*

For several months, her phone rings off the hook and applications pour through her letterbox – but none seem to match her qualifications. Then one day the doorbell rings. She opens the door to find a man, with no arms and no legs, lying on the welcome mat.

'Who are you?' she asked, perplexed. 'And what do you want?'

'Hi,' he replies, 'your search is over, for I'm the man of your dreams. I've got no arms – so I can't beat you up – and no legs, so I can't run away.'

'Hmm,' she says, unconvinced. 'What makes you think that you're so great in bed?'

He looks at her smugly. 'Well,' he grins. 'I rang the doorbell, didn't I?'

# And not a drop to drink ...

Following a dramatic escape from a burning freight vessel, two men are adrift
in a lifeboat. While rummaging through the boat's provisions, one of the men
finds an old lamp. Remembering old wives' tales of luck, he rubs the lamp
vigorously – and to the amazement of the castaways, a genie emerges from
the spout and offers them one wish.

Without giving much thought to the matter, the first man has an idea.

'I know,' he blurts out, 'Make the entire ocean into beer!'

The genie nods sagely, claps his hand – and, with a deafening crash, the
entire sea turns into the finest brew ever sampled by mortals. Simultaneously,
the genie vanished to his freedom. Only the gentle lapping of beer on the
hull disturbs the stillness as the two men considered their circumstances.

Beaming, the man turns around to find the other man looking at him
in disgust.

'Nice going!' he said after a long, tension-filled moment. 'Now we're going to
have to piss in the boat.'

# Flat out

After suffering years of torment from her friends, an extremely flat-chested woman finally decides to buy a bra, and goes to a high-class lingerie store.
'Excuse me,' she says to the assistant. 'Do you have a size 28AAAA bra?'
'Certainly not!' replies the saleswoman, haughtily – so the customer leaves and tries her luck in the next shop. Unfortunately, the response is the same: everywhere she goes she is rudely rebuffed. After trying eight lingerie stores, she angrily storms into a nearby bargain department store. Marching up to the sales clerk, she unbuttons her blouse.
'Do you have anything for these?' she yells.
The lady looks at her closely.
'I'm not sure,' she says. 'Have you tried Clearasil?'

# Hide and seek

It's been a particularly good day for a travelling salesman and he needs just one more sale to get his commission. He knocks at the door of the Smith family home. A small boy comes to the door, steps out onto the doorstep and whispers: 'What do you want?'
The salesman looks at the boy. 'Hello,' he says. 'Is your mummy home?'
'Yes,' the boy says, 'but she's very busy.'
'Okay,' says the salesman. 'What about your daddy. Can I have a quick word with him?'
'Nope,' whispers the boy. 'He's busy, too.'
The salesman pauses, but is desperate for his commission.
'What about your brothers and sisters? Do you have any?'
'Yes,' the little boy whispers, 'but they're all very busy as well.'
'Grandparents?' the salesman asks.
'Nope,' the boy says. 'They're tied up as well.'
'Are there any other adults in the house?' the salesman asks, exasperated.
'Yes,' the boy says. 'There's two firemen and a policeman here at the moment.'
'You mean your entire family, two firemen and a policeman are all in the house, but they're too busy to see me. What are they doing?'
'Looking for me,' the little boy whispers.

# You make me sick

Walking past an alleyway late one night, a policeman sees a tramp with two fingers shoved firmly up the arse of another tramp, who is kneeling on the floor.

'What the bloody hell do you two think you're playing at?' he asks.

The tramp doing the fingering stops, then looks up at the inquisitive copper to offer his explanation.

'It's quite simple really, officer,' he says. 'My good friend and companion here has drunk far too much today, and I am simply trying to make him sick it up.'

'Well,' the policeman says, 'sticking your fingers up his bumhole won't make him sick.'

'No, I know that,' says the fingering tramp. 'But sticking them in his mouth afterwards should do the trick.'

# Time's up

Concerned about his recent sexual performance, a man goes to see a doctor. After a couple of tests, the specialist sits him down for a quiet talk.

'I'm sorry,' the quack says, 'but it would appear that you have simply worn out your penis. By my reckoning you have 30 shags left, then that's it. Your sex life is over.'

The man walks home in a deep dark depression. His wife is waiting for him in their front room.

'Oh my God!' she cries when the man tells her of his misfortune. 'Thirty shags! We can't waste a single one of them. Every one must be special. Let's draw up a schedule right now.'

'I've already made a schedule on the way home,' the man says. 'And your name isn't on it.'

# Mum's the word

Kevin is driving over the Severn Bridge one day when he sees his girlfriend, Sharon, just about to throw herself into the water far below. Kevin slams on his brakes and shouts, 'Sharon! What do you think you're doing?'

Sharon turns around with a tear in her eye and says, 'Hello, Kevin. You got me pregnant, so now I'm going to kill myself.'

At this Kevin gets a lump in his throat.

'Sharon,' he says. 'Not only are you a great shag, but you're a real sport, too.'

## Free advice

After a chance meeting at St Andrews, Dave and Linda fall in love. There's a whirlwind romance, and over a candlelit dinner they discuss getting married. Dave, wanting to do the right thing, decides to come clean.

'Look, Linda,' he says, with a furrowed brow. 'I have to tell you – I'm a complete golf nut. I live, eat sleep and breathe golf. It's my life.'

'Well,' says Linda, 'Since you're being honest, so will I. I've been keeping a secret – I'm a hooker.'

Dave stares at her for a moment.

'I see,' he says, pensively. 'It's probably because you're not keeping your wrists straight when you make contact with the ball.'

## Overheard ... in an American emergency room

**Chandelier sign:** Behaviour exhibited when examining the cervix of a woman with pelvic inflammatory disease. It produces a pain so severe that the patient has to be scraped off the chandelier.

**Dash for cash:** Occurs when patients are transported to hospital by helicopters owned by private companies, which charge huge fees.

**Gomer:** Short for 'Get out of my emergency room.' Now applied to annoying senile patients.

**Gork:** Someone who has severe brain damage from a head injury.

**Negative wallet biopsy:** Refers to a private patient who has run out of money to pay for treatment.

**OTDMF:** Short for 'Out the door, Motherfucker'.

**PBAB:** 'Pine Box at the Bedside'. Refers to a patient about to croak.

**Pop drop:** When a family leave their demanding father at the ER.

**Q sign:** When the tongue falls out of the mouth and lolls to one side, forming the letter Q. Found in Gorks.

**A rock:** A patient who cannot be moved from the ER. Worst cases are known as 'diamonds'.

**Scut monkey:** A medical student forced to perform unpleasant duties.

**Stool magnet:** An especially unpopular medical student forced to perform even more unpleasant duties.

# You pays your money ...

The Queen visits a local hospital for the opening of a new wing, and is making a tour of the wards when she comes across a red-faced patient who's masturbating frantically.

'Good grief', HRH says. 'What on earth is this patient's problem?'

'Well, your Majesty', the ward sister says, 'he has a rare condition. He has to pull himself off at least eight times a day or his scrotum will swell like a balloon and eventually explode.'

'I see', the Queen says, and moves along to a small room, where the curtains are drawn around the bed. HRH royally draws back the drapes and is shocked to discover a nurse kneeling on the bed performing oral sex on a male patient.

'And what, may I ask', Elizabeth II says, 'is this man suffering from?'

'Oh', says the ward sister, 'he's got the same disease as the last man, only he's on BUPA.'

# A bit of a mouthful

It's a boring summer evening at Buckingham Palace, and after mindlessly teasing the corgis for an hour, the royals sit down for a quick game of 20 questions.

Soon, the Queen's turn arrives, and after a quick discussion the rest of the family returns – sniggering, for the object she has to guess is horse's cock.

'Off you go then, Lizzie', says Prince Phillip, trying not to laugh out loud.

'Er, is it bigger than a bread box?' says the monarch.

Snorting quietly, Princess Anne assures her that, yes, the item in question is bigger than a bread box.

'Umm... can I fit it in my mouth?' says the Queen.

Hiding his guffaws, Prince Charles replies no, she could not fit it in her mouth.

'Oh', says the Queen, 'Is it a horse's cock?'

# The frustrated grandmother

Patrick is walking down the street when he notices his grandfather sitting on his porch, in a rocking chair – with nothing on from the waist down.

'Grandpa', he asks, 'why are you sitting out here half-nude?'

The old man looked at him sheepishly.

'Well', he said. 'Last week I sat out here with no shirt on, and I got a stiff neck. This was your Grandma's idea.'

## An offer he can't refuse

A young man enters the chemists and nervously approaches the counter.
'Excuse me, miss, but could I talk to the owner?' he asks the girl behind
the counter.

'I am the owner,' says the young lady. 'Any business you wish to conduct in
here, you can talk to me about.'

'Well,' the young man replies, 'it's just that it's rather embarrassing.'

'Don't be so silly,' the chemist says. 'I've heard everything in my years behind
this counter, from genital warts to infected haemorrhoids.'

'Okay,' says the young fella with a blush. 'I've had this massive erection for
three days. It's like a steel rod and it doesn't hurt, but I'm afraid it'll never
go down. What do you think you can give me for it?'

'Wait here a moment,' the chemist says, and she turns away and walks into a
back room. A few minutes later she re-emerges and steps back up to the counter.
'My sister and I,' she says, 'have discussed the situation, and we'll give you
15 per cent of the business and an immediate cash pay-out of £20,000.'

## Economic realities

Ted begrudgingly agrees to go into town shopping with his wife. But after a
while he gets a bit bored and decides to nip off to the pub for a swift couple
of pints. Walking up the road towards the public house, he passes a prostitute
standing on the corner of the pavement. Bored by the prospect of another
dull night in front of the box with his old lady, he asks her how much she'd
want for penetrative sex.

'£20 for full sex,' the lady of the night replies.

'And what about a blow job?' the man asks.

'£15,' the whore answers.

'A quick hand-yank?' the man asks hopefully.

'Even that's a tenner,' the prozzie says.

'I've only got £3,' the man says. 'What can I have for that?'

'Oh Christ, I can't help you,' the tart says. 'You won't get an awful lot for £3.'

Dejected, the sad man leaves and goes back to meet up with his missus. They
finish off their shopping and walk arm-in-arm to the bus stop.

Who should be on the other side of the road but the streetwalker. And on
seeing the man, the whore bellows:

'I said you wouldn't get much for £3!'

## Quid pro quo

A man is relaxing in his back garden, sitting in the shade, sipping a beer and listening to the cricket on the radio. As he chills out, his wife struggles with a manual mower, pushing up and down the large lawn, sweating and red-faced. The man's next-door-neighbour sees the woman battling with the mower and shouts across the fence.

'You pathetic excuse for a man,' he yells, 'sitting there sipping your beer while your poor wife cuts the grass. You should be bloody well hung.'

'I am,' the man shouts back. 'That's why she's doing the grass.'

## Emergency medicine

A guy walks into a pharmacy and asks for a bottle of Viagra.

The pharmacist eyes him suspiciously.

'Do you have a prescription for that?' he asks.

'No,' says the guy, 'but will this picture of my wife do?'

# Getting your priorities right.

It's FA Cup Final day at Wembley Stadium and a young man is very disappointed when he finds his cheap seat is at the very rear of the stand, with a poor view of the pitch. A few seconds after kick-off he notices there is an empty seat near the front, so wanders up and casually sits down. After ten minutes he turns to the old man next to him.

'What kind of an idiot would book seats this good', he says, 'and not bother to turn up?'

'Actually', the old man says, 'the seat is mine. I reserved it for my wife, but she's now deceased. We've been coming to Cup Finals since 1960 – in fact, this is the first time I've ever been without her.'

'Oh my goodness', the young man says, 'I'm very sorry. But tell me, isn't there anyone else you could have given the seat to – a son or daughter, perhaps?'

'Oh, I couldn't do that, ' the old man says. 'They're all at the funeral.'

## Overheard ... at the Antarctic research station

**An Antarctic ten:** A woman who seems beautiful when you're stuck in the freezing isolation of Antarctica, but who's actually 'just a plane ride away from being ugly'.

**Apple:** A small, round prefabricated hut. Can be extended in to 'melon' or 'cucumber'.

**The banana belt:** An ironic term used to describe the slightly warmer climate of the Antarctic Peninsula.

**Big eye:** The terrible sleeplessness caused by living in 24-hour daylight.

**To blat:** To shoot, either with a camera or a gun.

**Bummock:** Geological slang for an underwater stalactite-like ice formation.

**The crud:** A flu-like illness that strikes when new crews arrive with fresh germs.

**Gash:** Non-biodegradable debris left on the ice by inconsiderate visitors.

**Hoosh:** A thick, hot stew made from dried meat and vegetables.

**The ice:** Antarctica

**Kodak poisoning:** The phenomenon of wildlife fleeing from tourists with cameras.

**Scradge:** A term applied to any type of food.

**A slushy:** Anyone who works in the kitchens.

## The amputee pool

Some amputees are at the swimming baths. One amputee, who has only one arm, bets the others that he can swim the length of the pool in under one minute. To prove it, he jumps in and begins to frantically churn through the water. Fifty-eight seconds later, to the amazement of the able-bodied swimmers, he is back at poolside.

Then a second amputee steps up. Although he has no arms and only one leg, he says he'll better the time, and jumps in. Fifty seconds later he is back to rapturous applause.

Next a man with no arms or legs jumps in, and with an incredible effort hauls himself through the water in 47 seconds. This gets a huge round of applause, until a head silences the crowd by announcing that he'll do the pool in 45 seconds. The head moves himself with his lips along to the pool's edge and dives in. Ten seconds later a spectator, realizing that the head is still underwater, jumps in to pull him out.

'What happened?' the spectator asks.

'Jesus,' the head splutters, 'what a time to get cramp.'

## Ask a stupid question ...

While walking down the street a man notices that a fellow pedestrian has a small orange instead of a head. Somewhat perturbed by this strange sight, he asks the man with the orange for a head how he came to have a fruit in place of his bonce.

'Well,' orange-head says, 'I found a lamp when I was out for a walk yesterday, and when I rubbed it a genie appeared. He granted me three wishes. First, I wished for £20 million.'

'And did you get it?' the man with the normal head asked.

'Yes,' the orange-headed man replied. 'So for my second wish I asked for a group of gorgeous willing women to appear and fulfil all my sexual fantasies. And that happened too.'

'My God, man,' the normal bloke said. 'What on earth did you ask for on your last wish?'

'Isn't it obvious?' said the man. 'I wished I had an orange for a head.'

## The ice-cream challenge

A guy walks into an ice-cream parlour and, bored with the taste of vanilla and strawberry, asks for a fish-and-chip-flavour cone. The owner rubs his chin and says, 'That's tricky. Give me ten minutes.'

Ten minutes later, the guy comes back and asks for his ice-cream. He licks it and says, 'Mmmm, that tastes great, just like a bag of chips. But what about the fish?'

The owner looks pleased and replies, 'Turn it around.' The guy does this, licks it and, lo and behold, it tastes like fish.

'Amazing,' he says. 'Now can I have one that tastes like faggots and peas?'

'That's tough,' says the ice cream man. 'Give me ten minutes.'

Ten minutes later, the guy comes back and picks up his ice cream.

'Mmmm, just like mushy peas,' he says. 'But what about the faggots?'

'Just turn it around,' says the gelati salesman.

'Oh yeah,' says the man. 'It's just like faggots. Now give me one that tastes like a woman's fanny.'

'That's difficult,' says the owner. 'Give me half an hour.'

So the man wanders off, returning 30 minutes later for his ice cream. He licks it and goes: 'Urghhhhh! Horrible! That tastes like shit!'

But the owner simply winks at him and says, 'Turn it around.'

## A blonde goes ice fishing

A blonde wanted to go ice fishing. She'd seen many books on the subject, and finally, after getting all the necessary items together, she made for the nearest frozen lake. After positioning her footstool, she started to make a circular cut in the ice. Suddenly, from the sky, a voice boomed:

'THERE ARE NO FISH UNDER THE ICE!'

Startled, the blonde moved further down the ice and began to cut yet another hole. Again, from the heavens, the voice bellowed:

'THERE ARE NO FISH UNDER THE ICE!'

The blonde, now quite worried, moved way down to the opposite end of the ice, set up her stool, and tried again to cut her hole. The voice came once more:

'THERE ARE NO FISH UNDER THE ICE!'

She stopped and looked skyward.

'Is that you, Lord?' she asked to the heavens.

'No,' the voice replied, 'This is the Ice-Rink Manager.'

## One on the house

A man walks into a bar and, in a strange strangulated high-pitched voice, orders a pint of beer. The barman gives him his glass of beer and asks him what is wrong with his throat. At this the man raises his head, tilts back his chin, and reveals a horrific scar.

The scar runs right across his throat, from ear to ear.

'Jesus!' the barman cries, 'That's nasty. How did you get that mate?'

The man takes a swig of his pint and then struggles to get out an answer: 'In the Falklands.'

'The Falklands?' the barman shouts. 'Then this drink is on the house. I have the utmost respect for you boys who put their lives on the line in that conflict.' At this, he slides over a glass of brandy to the scarred man.

'Muchas gracias,' the man says.

## Overheard ... rock climbers

**Airtime:** A very long fall. ('Jimmy must have done some serious airtime. He was nearly at the top when he lost his grip.')

**A Betty:** An attractive female climber, often seen with several male climbers following behind.

**A Bongie:** An environmentally friendly climber who uses old-fashioned equipment that doesn't damage rock. Taken from the sound he makes when he's climbing.

**Brain-bucket:** A helmet.

**To crater:** A fall right to the ground. ('John cratered badly. He's lying unconscious at the bottom.')

**Darwin in action:** An accident caused by incompetence or needless stupidity. ('Yeah, he got killed, but it was Darwin in action.')

**To Elvis:** The involuntary shaking of the legs which occurs when climbers' muscles suffer from over tension.

**To get chopped:** To be killed in a fall.

**Hating life:** What you're doing when you're climbing a face from which a fall could result in death.

**Logging (or launching a bag):** Having a shit whilst climbing (and usually letting it drop to the ground.)

**A party ledge:** A big, flat ledge where climbers can meet and rest.

**Pumping plastic:** Doing practice ascents on a gym climbing wall.

## Ballet lover

Various drinkers are enjoying an afternoon pint in the White Horse when a large, sweaty woman walks in, wearing a sleeveless sundress. She raises her right arm – revealing a big, hairy armpit – and points to rest of the customers. 'What man out there,' she booms, 'will buy a lady a drink?'

A deathly hush descends on the bar as the patrons try to ignore her – before a skinny little drunk pipes up. 'Bartender!' he says, slamming his hand on the bar, 'I want to buy that ballerina a drink!'

Baffled, the bartender pours a double whisky and the woman chugs it down. She wipes her mouth and, again, turns to the patrons. 'What man out there,' she roars, again revealing her hairy armpit, 'will buy a lady a drink?'

Once again the little drunk slaps his hand down on the bar and says, 'Bartender! I'd like to buy the ballerina another drink!'

After serving the lady her second drink, the bartender approaches the inebriated man. 'It's your business if you want to buy the lady a drink,' he says. 'But why do you call her a ballerina?'

The drunk squints at him. 'Sir,' he replies. 'In my eyes, any woman who can lift her leg up that high has to be a ballerina.'

# Amazing Grace

In ancient Rome, a Christian was being pursued by a lion. But as he ran through the city streets dodging back and forth, it became obvious that things were hopeless and the lion would catch him.

Clutching at straws, the hapless man turned suddenly, faced the beast and dropped to his knees.

'Lord', he prayed, desperately. 'Turn this lion into a Christian!'

Instantly, the lion fell to its knees and prayed, 'For what we are about to receive ...'

# Hedging your bets

Three men are sitting outside a maternity ward, waiting for their children to be born. One is from Liverpool, one is from Manchester and the third is a dreadlocked Rastafarian. After a few hours a doctor sees them.

'I've got some good news and some bad news', he tells them. 'The good news is that you're each the father of a healthy baby boy.'

The three men sigh thankfully.

'The bad news', he continues, 'is that we seem to have mixed the babies up and we don't know which child belongs to whom.'

The three new parents huddle together and come to the conclusion that each will recognize his own son. The Scouser steps forward and offers to claim his child first, and accompanies the doctor out of the waiting room.

He returns quickly with a black baby cradled in his arm.

The Rastafarian obviously claims the baby as his own, to which the Liverpudlian retorts:

'I don't care what you say, mate – one of the other two is a Manc.'

# Doggone

This man takes his sick dog to be seen by the vet. When it's his turn to be seen, the vet leads the poorly hound into the treatment room. He returns ten minutes later and says to the owner:

'Excuse me, sir, but could you say 'Ahhhh ...'.'

The dog's owner replies: 'Why do I have to say "Ahh ..."?'

The vet replies: 'Because your dog's dead.'

## The human statue

A woman is in bed with her lover when she hears her husband opening the front door. 'Hurry!' she says, 'Stand in the corner!' She quickly rubs baby oil all over him, before dusting him with talcum powder.

'Don't move until I tell you to,' she whispers. 'Just pretend you're a statue.'

Her husband enters the room. 'What's this, honey?' he enquires.

'Oh, it's just a statue,' she replies nonchalantly. 'The Smiths bought one for their bedroom. I liked it so much, I got one for us too.'

No more was said about the statue, not even later that night when they went to sleep. Around 2am, the husband got out of bed, went to the kitchen and returned with a sandwich and a glass of milk.

'Here,' he said to the 'statue'. 'Eat something. I stood like an idiot at the Smiths' for three days, and nobody offered me as much as a glass of water.'

## The hopeful shopper

A woman wanders into a chemist and glances at the display counter.

'Excuse me,' she asks the pharmacist after a few moments. 'Do you sell extra-large condoms?'

'Yes we do,' comes the reply. 'Would you like to buy some?'

'No,' says the woman, looking around. 'But do you mind if I wait around until someone does?'

## A point of principle

A man walks up to a woman seated in a bar.

'Excuse me,' he says, 'I'm doing a survey. Would you have sex with a man you didn't know for one million dollars?'

The woman mulls over the proposition for a minute.

'Yes,' she replies. 'I would sleep with a man I don't know for a million dollars.'

The man nods. 'OK then – would you sleep with me for fifty cents?'

Insulted, the woman snorts.

'Of course not!' she cries. 'How could you ask me such a thing?'

The man looks at her slyly.

'Well, we've already established that you're a whore,' he replies. 'Now I'm just haggling over the price.'

## Pieman Prat

A bloke walks into a pub with a meat and potato pie balanced on his head. He walks up to the barman and says, 'Can I have a pint of bitter, please.' 'Certainly,' says the barman, and starts pulling a pint. But he can't resist asking: 'You do realize, sir, you have a meat and potato pie on your head?' The bloke says: 'Yes, I always have a meat and potato pie on my head on a Wednesday.'

'Ah!' says the barman. 'But today is Tuesday!'

'Oh no,' says the bloke. 'I must look like a right twat.'

## Overheard ... on a yacht

**Arsehole:** A small kink in a rope that prevents it from sliding through a pulley. As in, 'It won't move. There must be an arsehole in the line.'

**Ballast:** A crew member who knows nothing about boating and who is proving a serious danger to everyone else on board.

**To check the tension of the backstay:** To piss off the back of the boat while at sea.

**Floating clotheslines:** What professional fisherman and powerboat drivers call the boats of amateur weekend sailors.

**Furniture store:** A boat with interior decoration designed to impress, but which actually slows the boat down.

**Hard water:** Rocks.

**Harvey Wallbanger:** A yacht hired by amateurs, who have a tendency to crash in to docks.

**Head dweller:** Someone who gets seasick easily.

**Hydraulic sandwiches:** Beer carried aboard ship.

**Rail meat:** A novice sailor, whose only practical use is to sit on the side of the boat to balance it during a storm.

**Squid:** What sailors call marina staff – especially those who are paid to clean the boats of customers.

**Squirt boats:** The name given by sail-driven vessel owners to powerboats.

## Bear squared

How do you make a bear cross?
Just nail two bears together.

# The randy rooster

A poultry farmer wakes up to find that his elderly rooster has died in the night.
With 200 hens and no chicks, he decides he needs a new rooster.
He goes to the local market and spies Randy, a prize specimen of a rooster:
tall, lean with a wild look in his eye.
'He'll service every hen you've got, no problem,' says the owner. 'He's a
sex machine.'
The farmer decides Randy is worth the extra money, and takes him back to
the barn. The effect is amazing – Randy bursts out of his carrying box, and
immediately starts on the startled chickens in the coop.
Shocked, the farmer grabs the crazed rooster and holds him back.
'Whoah there, Randy,' he says. 'You'll wear yourself out, and there are a lot of
chickens left.'
But as soon as the farmer releases him, he's away again – the feathers flying
as his little chicken behind pumps away. Worse, he then sprints out of the barn
and sees a flock of geese. As he finishes, the farmer watches in disbelief as he
then starts on the pigs, then is off into the field after the cows.
Within hours Randy has had half the animals on the farm, and the farmer goes
to bed – concerned his expensive rooster won't even last the day. Sure enough,
the farmer wakes the next day to find Randy dead as a doornail, lying in the
middle of the farmyard. As buzzards circle ominously overhead, the farmer
says: 'Oh Randy, I told you to pace yourself, but you just wouldn't listen.'
The rooster opens one eye, and looks towards the buzzards.
'Shhh,' he says, 'they're getting closer ...'

# Fame!

After days of abdominal pain, a man goes to the doctor for some tests.
Returning a few weeks later, he asks for the results.
'Hmm,' says the doc, looking up from his paperwork. 'I have some good news
and some bad news.'
The patient is visibly concerned. 'I suppose I'd better have the good news first.'
'Well,' sighs the doctor. 'We're going to name a disease after you.'

# Never trust a man in a white coat

About to undergo a minor operation, a beautiful young girl is laid on a gurney by a nurse and left alone in the corridor. While she's away, a young man in a white coat approaches, takes the sheet away and starts examining her naked body. He walks away and talks to another man in a white coat. The second man comes over and does the same examinations. When a third man starts examining her body, the girl starts growing impatient.

'All these examinations are great,' she says. 'But are you starting the operation?' The first man shrugs his shoulders.

'I have no idea. We're just painting the corridor.'

# The pushy stranger

Brian is asleep in bed with his wife when there's a loud knocking at the front door. He rolls over, looks at the clock and sees that it's 3am.

'Sod that for a game of soldiers,' he says and goes back to sleep.

Five minutes later the knocking starts again, this time louder.

'Aren't you going to answer that,' mumbles his wife.

Sighing, Brian drags himself out of bed, goes downstairs and opens the door. A man is standing there, getting soaked in the pouring rain.

'Excuse me, mate,' he says, 'But you couldn't give us a push, could you?'

'A push?' says Brian, 'It's three in the morning, and I was asleep – piss off.'

He slams the door, goes back to bed and tells his wife what happened.

'Brian, you are a dick. Remember that night we broke down in the rain on the way to pick up the kids, and you had to knock at that man's door to get us started again? What would have happened if he'd told us to piss off?'

Sheepishly, Brian gets dressed and goes downstairs. Opening the door, he can't see the stranger so he shouts: 'Mate – do you still want a push?'

'Yes please, mate,' comes the reply.

Brian peers into the darkness.

'So where are you then?'

'I'm over here on the swings.'

# Bad reception

What's got four legs and goes 'Shhhhhhhhh'?
Rod Hull's telly.

## What a winker

George had gained an interview for a job at a top City company, but unfortunately, he had a problem with one of his eyes – it winked constantly. 'We'd love to take you on,' said the managing director, 'But that winking is too distracting.'

'Wait! I can make it stop by taking two aspirin,' said George. Reaching into his pocket, he then pulled out a dozen condom packets and placed them on the deck before finding two aspirin. He took the tablets and winking instantly stopped. 'That's all well and good,' said the MD said, 'But we don't condone womanizing here.'

'No, no. You've got it all wrong,' said George. 'Have you ever asked for aspirin at the chemists while you're winking?'

## Woman's work

While flying from London to New York at 36,000 feet, a Boeing 747 suddenly develops engine trouble and starts plummeting towards the Atlantic. As she realizes what's going on, the head stewardess crashes into the pilots' cabin, stands in front of the captain and rips off her blouse, saying:

'Captain, make me feel like a woman one more time before I die!'

The pilot rips his shirt off and says: 'Here you go then, love – iron this.'

## Payback time

Two lawyers are standing in the queue at the bank one busy lunchtime, when a man walks in brandishing a handgun. The thief makes his way along the queue of customers and tells them all to empty their pockets, take off their jewellery and put it in the sack he is holding.

As he gets closer and closer to the pair of lawyers, one of them takes his wallet out of his back pocket, opens it, and hands his companion a crisp £50 note. 'What's this?' the friend asks.

'Oh,' says the first lawyer, 'it's the £50 I owe you.'

## Swing low, sweet chariot

What does a 75-year-old woman have between her knees that a 25-year-old doesn't?

Her nipples.

## Miracle worker

Jesus and Saint Paul are sitting in Heaven, talking about all the pollution on Earth and wondering what can be done about mankind's filthy ways. Jesus says he's going to pop down to Skegness to see the situation for himself, and Paul agrees to join him.

When they get there, Jesus asks what the huge metal pipe is for. Paul tells him it's used to take human waste out to sea where the muck kills dolphins, so Jesus decides to take action and strides out across the waves. Walking alongside, Paul is soon knee-deep in filthy water, while Jesus scoots along on top of the sea. Ever hopeful of some help he slogs on, and Jesus keeps walking on water ... but soon the water is up to Paul's chin.

'Master,' he calls, 'I will follow you anywhere, but I'm up to my neck in shitty water and I think I'm going to drown.'

At this Jesus stops walking and looks at Paul.

'Well,' he says, 'why don't you just walk on the pipe like me, you silly prick?'

## Mother knows best

Young Mary has just got married but is quite a traditionalist, and is still a virgin on her wedding night. As a result, her husband Tony agrees to let Mary's mother stay over to quell any fears the girl might have. On the big night the young couple go upstairs and Tony takes off his shirt to reveal a hairy chest. Young Mary runs down to her mother.

'Mother!' she cries. 'Tony has a hairy chest!'

'It's all right,' her mother says. 'All good men have hairy chests.'

Mary goes back upstairs and Tony takes his trousers off to reveal hairy legs. Again Mary runs down to her mother.

'Mother!' she wails. 'Tony has hairy legs!'

'Don't worry, my child,' her mother says. 'All good men have hairy legs.'

Mary goes back upstairs, and Tony takes off his shoes and socks to reveal a left foot with no toes. Again the naive young girl runs to her mother.

'Oh, mother,' she moans, 'Tony only has a foot and a half.'

At this, her mother sits her down on the sofa.

'You stay down here, little one,' she says. 'This is a job for your mother.'

## Shouldn't they be in water?

Jean goes round to visit her next-door neighbour Sally, where she notices some freshly cut flowers lying on the sideboard.

'Are these from your husband?' she asks.

Sally nods, and puts the kettle on.

'I suppose you'll be lying flat on your back with your legs spread later tonight' Jean says.

'Oh no,' says Sally. 'I'll just put them in a vase.'

## Hot dog

A well-to-do lady is at the vets one day with her two dachshunds – one male, the other female. Whilst examining them both, the vet enquires as to whether the bitch has 'been dressed', or the dog given the snip.

In a casual tone the lady replies, 'Oh, that's not necessary. The bitch stays up the stairs and the dog stays downstairs'.

'And how does that prevent them from mating,' asks the vet?

'Have you ever seen a dachshund trying to climb stairs with a hard-on?' replies the lady.

## The 20th anniversary

A wife wakes up in the middle of the night to find her husband missing. Hearing sobbing from the living room, she goes down to find her husband crying his eyes out. 'What's the matter?' the woman asks.

'You remember 20 years ago,' the man sobs, 'when I got you pregnant and your father said I had to marry you or go to jail?'

'Sure, honey,' the kindly wife replies. 'So what?'

'Well,' the man gasps through desperate sobs, 'I would have been released tonight.'

## Overheard ... birdwatchers

**Birders:** A term birdwatchers use to refer to themselves.

**A dipper:** A bird you travel a long way to see, only to find it's flown away by the time you get there. As in: 'I went all the way to Scotland, but it was a dipper.'

**Gashawk:** aeroplane, especially one that scares the birds away.

**Triple B (or BBB):** Bolted before the binoculars. Indicates the bird's disappearance before the birder gets close.

**A granny birder:** Someone who only knows and spots the most common birds. So called because they act like old women getting excited about chaffinches.

**Hawkoreagle:** An unidentified bird of prey.

**Jizz:** The bird's movement pattern in flight, from which it can often be identified. As in: 'That's definitely a wood duck. Look at its jizz.' Comes from the RAF abbreviation 'GIS', which stands for General Impression and Shape.

**LBJ:** Little Brown Job. Any dull bird the birder can't be bothered to identify.

**Owl Prowl:** Night-time birding.

**Pishing:** The noise a birder makes to try and get birds to move out into the open. Sounds like, 'Psshh, psshh.'

**PTT:** Pre-tick tension. The anxiety a birdwatcher goes through when anticipating seeing a new bird.

**Punkies:** Young birds, so called because of their distinctive plumage.

**Ring 'em and fling 'em:** What birders do during scientific studies of birds in a particular area. Each bird is examined, given a tag and released.

**Stringy:** Used to describe a dubious sighting, especially if it is suspected that the birder has completely made it up.

**Tick:** The bird. Which can then be ticked off the list. Also 'Megatick': a really rare or sought-after bird.

## Ultimate sacrifice

While serving a life imprisonment, a murderer breaks free and goes on the run. He breaks into a house near the prison and ties up the young couple he finds in the bedroom. Bound to a chair, the young husband is helpless as the psychopath gets onto the bed where his wife is tied and starts to nuzzle her neck. After a while he gets up and leaves the room – and the husband takes his chance to bounce the chair across the room to his young wife.

'Darling,' he hisses. 'I saw him kissing you. He can't have seen a woman in years. Please cooperate: if he wants to have sex, just go along with it and even pretend you like it. Whatever you do, don't fight him or make him mad. Our lives may depend on it!'

'Darling', says the wife, spitting out her gag, 'I'm so relieved you feel that way. He wasn't kissing me ... he was whispering to me that he thinks you're really cute and asked if we kept the Vaseline in the bathroom.'

## Memory lapse

An elderly man walks into a brothel and tells the madam he would like a really young girl for the night. The old steamer gives him a puzzled look and asks the fellow how old he is.

'Why,' the man says, 'I'm 98 years old.'

'Ninety-eight!' the madam exclaims. 'Don't you realize you've had it?'

'Oh,' he says, 'how much do I owe you, then?'

## A job well done

On their 30th wedding anniversary, a couple decided to go back to the same hotel where they spent their blissful first night together. Just as she had 30 years before, the wife emerges from the bathroom totally nude and stands seductively in front of him.

'Tell me, darling,' she purrs. 'What were you thinking 30 years ago when I came out of the bathroom like this?'

'I took one look at you,' says her husband, eyeing her thoughtfully. 'And thought I'd like to screw your brains out and suck your boobs dry.'

'And what are you thinking now, baby?' she asked huskily.

'Hmmm,' he mulls. 'I'm thinking I did a pretty good job of it.'

## Mental arithmetic

Timmy comes home with his report card, and his mother is angry to read he's received another D in maths.

'I warned you,' she chastises him, 'If you didn't get better grades this term, I was going to have to send you to the Catholic school.'

So the Timmy was packed off the local convent – from where, a term later, his mother is overjoyed to see him come home with an A in maths.

'I can't believe it!' she exclaims. 'What happened at Catholic school to cause such an improvement?'

'Well, I knew those people weren't kidding around,' he says, pulling off his satchel, 'when I walked into class the first day and saw that guy nailed to the plus sign.'

## Hot shit

With a screech of brakes, an ambulance pulls up at the local casualty ward and a hippie is wheeled out on a gurney. The doctor questions his long-haired colleagues. 'So what was he doing then?' says the physician. 'Acid? Cannabis?' 'Sort of', replies one of the hippies, nervously thumbing his caftan. 'But we ran out of gear, so I made a home-made spliff.'

'And what was in that?' replies the doctor.

'Um, I kind of raided my girlfriend's spice rack', says the hippie. 'There was a bit of cumin, some turmeric and a little paprika.'

'Well that explains it', the doctor replies, looking at them gravely. 'He's in a korma.'

## Overheard ... on the set of a game show

**A Bambi:** A contestant who freezes when the cameras starts rolling. Based on the reaction of frightened animals blinded by headlights.

**Corrective surgery:** The process of weeding out unsuitable, undesirable or just downright weird potential contestants or audience members.

**Cue the Kleenex:** The stage direction given when an excitable contestant is about to win the jackpot. It usual involves a close up on the contestants face in case they blub.

**DAS:** 'Dull as shit.' Applied to any contestant lacking in charisma and with no interesting anecdotes to tell.

**To dumb off:** What the host does when he has to reveal the answer to a question himself because none of the contestants know it.

**Elbow-grabber:** The beautiful female assistant whose job consists entirely of ferrying contestants on and off set.

**God:** The member of the production team the host defers to when he wants to know if an answer is acceptable.

**The Idiot:** The term used by some producers to refer to the host.

**Judases:** Audience members who can't resist shouting out the answers.

**Lovely parting gifts:** The cheap trinkets given to losing contestants to remind them of their time on the show.

**The march of shame:** What the elbow grabber does when she drags an eliminated contestant off the set.

**A tornado:** A brilliant contestant who trounces all the opposition and walks away with a whole stack of prizes.

## Look right, look left

A middle-aged woman has a heart attack and is rushed to hospital on the very cusp of death. After being given a quick jolt of the defibrillator the woman is revived, and she tells the doctors that she had a near-death experience.

'I saw God, ' the beaming woman explains. 'He told me that it was not my time and that I had a good 30 to 40 years of life left on this earth.'

The woman makes a good recovery from her trauma, and as a result of her meeting with God she decides to really enjoy her life. She decides she wants to completely revamp her image and checks into a clinic for the works: face job, liposuction, boob job and hair colouring. After a few weeks to recover the makeover is complete, and the woman checks out and walks along the street feeling bright and breezy and full of hope for the future. She steps out at a zebra crossing and a lorry ploughs into her, killing her instantly.

The woman goes up to Heaven and stands in front of God in a fury. 'I thought you said I had a good 30 or 40 years left!' she cries indignantly.

'What can I say?' God says, obviously embarrassed. 'I didn't recognize you.'

## Undercover operator

A man and his wife are driving home in their expensive new car one night when they both get horny, and decide to christen the sparkling motor with a shag. Pulling into a lay-by they get down to business, but soon realize their nice new motor's actually too small for the amount of erotic manoeuvring they want to do. The guy suggests they climb out and have a go under the car, which he promises his wife will provide ample clearance for his heaving buttocks, so the couple slip under the pristine vehicle and go at it like the clappers. In fact, they're enjoying themselves so much that they don't notice when a policeman comes over and taps the man on the back of his exposed legs.

'What do you think you're doing?' the copper asks the man.

'I'm just fixing my car,' the chap calmly replies.

'No you're not!' the policeman says through hysterical laughter. 'You're having sex in public, and I'm going to nick you for indecent exposure.'

'How do you know I'm lying?' the indignant man asks.

'Well,' the copper replies, 'for a start you're facing downwards on top of a naked woman. Secondly, I don't see any tools anywhere. And thirdly, your car was stolen five minutes ago.'

# The baffled parrot

A magician gets a job on the Titanic. During his first performance, the captain's loud-mouthed parrot shouts out, 'It's up his sleeve! It's up his sleeve!' and ruins his act. The next night, the parrot again jumps in, yelling, 'It's in his pocket!' and, 'He's swapped them over!'

Throughout the whole voyage, no matter how good a trick the magician does, the parrot always spoils it.

Then the boat hits the fateful iceberg and sinks into the freezing depths. The magician manages to get into a lifeboat, and is joined by the parrot. At first, the bird refuses to talk, but after two weeks adrift, it finally cracks.

'Okay', it says, 'you win. What have you done with the ship?'

# The boogieman

A barrister walks into a bar and sits down next to a drunk. Soon the lawyer realizes the drunk is carefully studying something in his hand and holding it up to the light.

'What do you have there?' asks the curious barrister.

The drunk shakes his head.

'Damned if I know. It looks like plastic and it feels like rubber.'

'Let me take a look,' says the lawyer, and rolls it between his fingers.

'Yeah, you're right,' he says. 'It does look like plastic and feel like rubber, but I don't know what it is. Where did you get it?'

The drunk looks at him. 'Out of my nose.'

# Hungry bum

A man goes to the doctor's and says, 'Doctor, I really need some help. I can't seem to get an erection.'

The doctor examines him carefully and suggests a number of remedies – all to no avail.

'Herbal remedies, Viagra, hydraulic pumps – nothing seems to work,' says the man.

'Well,' the doctor says, 'There is a last-ditch option. Scientists at the local hospital are doing some experimental work with elephant muscle tissue transplants. But I have to warn you, they are not sure of the side-effects.'

The guy thinks for minute: 'Look, doctor, I'm desperate. I'll do anything.'

So he's booked in for the operation, it all goes perfectly – and six weeks later the man has recovered enough to try his luck with a gorgeous secretary in his office. So they're sitting at dinner, enjoying their starters when the man starts to get horny. Sure enough, he's getting hard – and thinks his troubles are finally over.

Suddenly, the zip on his trousers splits open, his knob bursts out onto the table, grabs a bread roll out of the secretary's hand and disappears under the table again.

The woman is amazed. 'Wow,' she says, 'Can you do that again ... later?'

The man looks thoughtful.

'Well,' he says, 'I don't know if I can fit another bread roll up my arse.'

# Sweet smell of success

Sitting at home one night with his wife, a man is casually tossing peanuts into the air and catching them in his mouth. As the couple take in the latest episode of Watchdog the man loses concentration for a split second, and a peanut goes into his ear. He tries to get the nut out, but succeeds only in forcing the thing in awfully deep.

After a few hours of fruitless rooting the couple decide to go to the hospital, but on their way out of the front door they meet their daughter coming in with her boyfriend. The boyfriend takes control of the situation: he tells them he's studying medicine and that they're not to worry about a thing. He then sticks two fingers up the man's nose and asks him to blow – and lo, the nut shoots from the ear and out across the room.

As the daughter and her boyfriend go through to the kitchen to make a pot of tea, the man and his wife sit down to discuss their luck.

'So', the wife says, 'what do you think he'll become after he qualifies? A GP or a surgeon?'

'Well, ' says the man, rubbing his nose, 'by the smell of his fingers, our son-in-law.'

# Smells fishy ...

A man is fishing at his local pool when a fellow angler sets up beside him. After a while spent chatting, the newcomer reveals he got married the day before and is on his honeymoon with his new wife.

'So why are you fishing and not with your new wife?' says the first man.

'I just love fishing,' comes the reply. 'So far I've been fishing all day and all night. I love it!'

'Well, it's nothing to do with me,' says the first man, 'but aren't you missing out on fantastic sex with your new bride at home?'

'I was going to, but she's got gonorrhoea,' he answers.

'Well it *is* your honeymoon – couldn't you give her one up the arse?'

'I was going to, but she's got diarrhoea.'

'In that case,' says the first, 'she could at least give you a blow job.'

'I was going to ask her but she's got cold sores and warts all over her mouth,' comes the answer.

The first man is confused: 'Gonorrhoea, diarrhoea, cold sores and warts – Jesus, why the hell did you marry her?'

'Great maggots,' comes the reply.

## Keep your hat on

On his daily beat, a policeman notices an old lady standing on a corner as a wind whistles through the street. She's clutching her hat firmly to her head as the wind lifts her skirt, showing her pants to the world.

'Look lady,' the cop says, 'while you're holding on to your bonnet, you're showing the whole world your package down there.'

'Listen, sonny,' the unctuous old mare says to the copper. 'What they're getting an eyeful of is 90 years old. This hat, however, is brand new.'

## Overheard ... in the legal profession

**Bag ladies:** Women who bring bags of their husband's bank statements into the solicitor's office, hoping to make a packet from divorcing them.

**Burnt toast jurisprudence:** An unusually harsh sentence passed down by a judge who's 'having a bad day'.

**Blue-hair case:** A lawsuit involving an old-age pensioner suing someone after slipping and injuring themselves on their property.

**Come-to-Jesus meeting:** What takes place when a lawyer explains that his client has no chance of winning a case and should settle out of court.

**Dumper truck:** A lawyer who promises to defend his client to the last, then pleads him guilty as soon as the case gets to court.

**Mr Green:** The codeword used by defence lawyers to tell the judge they are waiting for payment before proceeding with the case. As in, 'I'm waiting for the witness Mr Green to appear, Your Honour.'

**A nail-and-mail:** What happens when a witness can't be contacted in person. A subpoena is served by nailing it on the witness's front door then sending them a duplicate by post.

**To piss backwards:** When a witness in court contradicts a statement he gave earlier to police.

**To sandbag:** When the prosecution withholds evidence from the defence to try and surprise them in court.

**Shopper:** A soon-to-be-divorced woman with no job, skills or savings. As in 'Mrs Jones is a shopper, so we'll need to ask for big alimony payments.'

**Treasure maps:** Financial records used by a divorce lawyer to find the hidden assets of a client's husband.

**Walking the dog:** What a barrister is doing when he goes to court knowing he's going to lose the case.

## Safe sex

A beautiful woman is driving back to the city when her sports car breaks
down. Desperate, she wanders over the fields and spies a farmhouse, where
she knocks on the door.

'Oh, thank God,' she says, after the farmer answers. 'My car's broken down –
could I stay the night until someone comes out tomorrow?'

The farmer eyes her suspiciously.

'Well, okay,' he says. 'But don't mess with my two sons, Jed and Jake.'

Behind him, two strapping young men appear, smiling sheepishly. The woman
agrees, but after going to the guest-room, she can't stop thinking about the
two young bucks in the next room. Throwing caution to the wind, she quietly
tip-toes across.

'Jake! Jed!' she whispers. 'Would you like me to teach you the ways of
the world?'

'Huh?' comes the reply.

'The only thing is,' says the woman, 'I don't want to get pregnant – so you'll
have to wear these condoms.' Beaming, the boys agree – and soon embark on
a glorious night of three-way passion.

Forty years later, Jed and Luke are sitting on their front porch, fondly remembering their erotic experience.

'It was fantastic,' says Jed. 'But I do have one question.'

'Oh?' says Jake.

His brother frowned. 'Well, do you really care if that woman gets pregnant?'

'Nope,' says Jake, thoughtfully. 'I reckon not.'

'Me, neither,' says Jed. 'Let's take these things off.'


## **Eyecatching**

Worried that it might be raining, a bloke in an apartment complex sticks his head out the window to check. As he does so a glass eye falls into his hand. He looks up in time to see a beautiful young woman looking down.

'Is this yours?' he asks.

'Yes,' she replied, 'would you bring it up for me?' The man agrees.

Upon his arrival she is profuse in her thanks and offers him a drink. They sit and chat for a couple of hours, before she says:

'I'm about to have dinner. There's plenty – would you care to join me?'

The man leaps at the offer and has a fantastic meal. As they carry their dishes to the kitchen the woman says, 'I've had a marvellous evening. Would you like to spend the night with me?'

The man hesitates, then asks, 'Do you act like this with every man you meet?'

'No,' she replies, 'only with those who catch my eye.'


## **Flat out**

An embarrassed man visits the doctor and confesses that he fears he has something wrong with his sexual organs. He takes out his knob, which is covered with scabby sores, dead skin and a weeping yellow discharge.

The doctor winces, but after examining him thoroughly, he sighs and tells the man he has GASH.

'GASH, doctor? What the hell's that?' says the man.

'It's a combination of Gonorrhoea, AIDS, Syphilis and Herpes.'

'Oh, God,' the young man says, 'Is there anything that can be done for me?'

'Yes,' replies the doctor, 'but it involves immediate hospitalization, and feeding you a special diet of Dover sole, pizza and pancakes.'

'Dover sole, pizza and pancakes? Why those in particular?'

'Because it's the only things we can get under the door.'

## Sucking a lemon

Distraught and guilty, a woman goes to her priest to seek forgiveness. 'Forgive me father,' she says, 'for I have sinned.'

'What is it you have done, my child?' asks the priest.

'Last night my boyfriend made love to me seven times,' the young lassie says.

'You must go home,' says the priest, 'and suck the juice from seven lemons.'

'Will that cleanse me of my sins?' the girl asks.

'No,' the holy man replies, 'but it'll wipe that smug grin off your face.'

## Overheard ... missionaries

**To burn:** To accidentally catch a glimpse of the private parts of another missionary.

**To DRT:** 'Develop a relationship of trust.' To get the conversion target on your side.

**Fetch:** The word missionaries use when they don't want to swear. 'Oh fetch, I just don't want to call on that house again'.

**Gaggies:** Very badly-cooked biscuits which help keep hunger at bay when knocking on doors.

**The grape sheet:** The list of houses to be visited and phone numbers to be called. One grape sheet is given to every missionary.

**Jay Vees:** Jehovah's Witnesses.

**OP:** 'Off the programme.' Applied to anything not considered conductive to the mission, as in: 'The group leader's behaviour was most definitely OP'.

**The holy broom:** The sack. As in, 'The elder was caught fornicating and got given the holy broom'.

**To be pasteurized:** See 'the holy broom'.

**To be peeped:** When a householder looks through the peephole in the front door before opening it.

**Phoney honker:** A missionary who's along for the ride and doesn't really believe in God.

**Trunky papers:** A communiqué from mission headquarters telling you to return to base.

## Pillow talk

A man comes home after a hard day's work, looking forward to relaxing. He pours himself a glass of wine, eats a delicious meal cooked by his wife and goes upstairs to his bedroom, where he and his wife have separate beds. His wife follows him up a minutes later.

'Honey-woney,' the man says, 'I just want to thank you for fixing me such a delicious meal. I am blessed to have such a wife as you.'

He then turns out the light and tries to sleep.

After several minutes he finds he can't nod off.

'Sweetie pie,' he calls out, 'I'm lonely.' His wife gets out of bed and makes her way across the room, but she slips, falls and bangs her nose.

'Did my little bunny fall and hurt her nosey-wosey?' the man asks, as his wife climbs into bed with him. There follows a three-hour session of hardcore sex. When the couple have finished, the wife heads back over to her own bed, and as she goes she slips up a second time.

'Clumsy bitch,' the man mutters.

## Silver service

The Lone Ranger and Tonto are enjoying a quiet beer or two in the Dead Gulch Saloon one afternoon when a man bursts through the swinging doors.

'Which one of you men owns that white horse outside?' the panting stranger asks the pair.

'I do,' says the Lone Ranger. 'Why do you ask, hombre?'

'The animal's collapsed,' the man says. 'I think he might be dead.'

The three men rush outside and see that Silver is, indeed, lying in the red dirt of Main Street. The Lone Ranger drips water into the poor horse's mouth, and Silver appears to perk up a little bit.

'It's just heat exhaustion,' the Lone Ranger says. 'Tonto, will you run in circles around Silver for a while? I think the breeze will help to get him back on his feet.'

Tonto begins sprinting around the horse, and the Lone Ranger goes back into the saloon to finish his beer. But just a few minutes later, another man comes bursting through the swinging doors.

'Who owns that white horse outside?' the man asks.

'Oh, dammit,' the Lone Ranger says. 'What's wrong with him now?'

'Nothing partner,' the man says. 'It's just that you left your injun running.'

# Natural reaction

On walking into his local, Dave sees his mate Jeff looking depressed at the bar, and asks him what's wrong.

'Well,' replies Jeff, 'You know that gorgeous girl at work? The one who gives me an erection every time I saw her?'

'Yes,' replies Dave with a smile.

'Well,' says Jeff, straightening up, 'I finally plucked up the courage to ask her out, and she agreed.'

'That's great!' says Dave, 'when are you going out?'

'I went to meet her this evening,' continues Jeff. 'I was worried about getting a hard-on so I taped my todger to my leg, so it wouldn't show. But when I got to her house she was wearing the sheerest tiniest dress you ever saw.'

'And what happened then?' asked Dave.

Jeff huddles over the bar again. 'I kicked her in the face.'

# Tough Decision

Jim is walking down the street when his mate Dave rides up on a shiny new bicycle.

'Where did you get such a fantastic bike?' he asks him.

Dave replies, 'Well, yesterday I was walking along minding my own business when a beautiful woman rode up on this bike. She threw the bike to the ground, took of all her clothes and said, "Take what you want." So I did.'

Jim nods: 'Good choice – I don't think the clothes would have fitted.'

# No way to win

A guy receives a phone call from his local surgery telling him there's been a terrible mix-up with his wife's medical tests. 'We don't know if she's the one with herpes or a heart condition,' apologizes the doctor.

'Oh my god, what can I do?' asks the guy.

'Well,' suggests the doctor, 'send her out jogging and if she comes back don't fuck her!'

# Lassie learns a lesson

This dog walks into the butcher's shop one afternoon, with a large basket in his mouth. He jumps up onto the counter, puts the basket down and pulls a neatly folded note from within. The butcher opens the note. It reads: 'Please give the dog 1 lb of Cumberland sausages, 1 lb of smoky back bacon, half a dozen lamb chops, 2 lb of rump steak and three slices of gala pie.'

The butcher weighs out the goods and puts them in the basket.

'That'll be £16.54, please,' he says to the dog, who takes a purse from the basket and counts out the exact money with his mouth. The dog then nods his head in thanks, takes the basket back in his mouth, and leaves the shop.

The butcher is stunned by the brilliance of this display – and even more so a week later, when the same thing happens. A further week passes, and the same thing happens again, but this time the butcher shuts up the shop and follows the clever little dog as he trots through the streets. He keeps behind the hound as he makes his way across busy intersections, always observing the Highway Code, until finally the dog walks up to a house, places the basket on the ground and knocks on the door with his paw. The butcher is stunned by the intelligence of the canine.

The door opens and a man in a stained wife-beater vest comes out and starts kicking the dog all over the pavement. The butcher is horrified and runs to restrain the man.

'Stop!' he cries. 'Why are you beating such a clever little animal?'

'He has to learn,' the man replies. 'This is the third time this month he's forgotten his keys.'

## Teaching her the ropes

A Texan and his bride ask the hotel desk clerk for a room, telling him they just got married that morning.

'Congratulations!' says the clerk. 'Luckily, all our suites are still available. Would you like the bridal?'

'Naw thanks,' says the cowboy. 'I reckon I'll just hold her by the ears till she gets the hang of it.'

## The zebra and the bull

A farmer goes to a livestock auction, but hasn't bought anything by the time the last lot comes up. Not wanting to go home empty-handed, he buys the beast, a female zebra, takes her home and sticks her in a field, not really knowing what to do with the animal. The zebra herself is also fairly bemused. She walks up to a chicken and asks the bird what it does around the farm.

'Oh, I just peck at the loose corn on the ground,' the chicken says. 'And lay eggs for the farmer.'

'I can't do that,' the zebra says, and walks off to talk to the pig.

'What do you do?' the zebra asks the pig.

'Well,' the pig says, 'I eat rotting vegetables and sit in the mud getting fat all day.'

'I don't fancy that much,' says the zebra, and trots off to talk to the bull, who's sporting a massive erection.

'And what exactly do you do around here?' the zebra asks the excited bull.

'Well,' the bull says, 'take your pyjamas off and I'll show you.'

## The wheelbarrow

Months of sexual frustration force a couple to seek advice from a counsellor. After a brief chat with the pair to find out the source of their anguish, the therapist suggests some new sex positions to spice up their nights.

'For example, he suggests, 'why not try the barrow? Lift her by the legs, penetrate and off you go.'

The couple then head off home. Champing at the bit, the husband suggests trying the barrow.

'Okay,' the wife agrees, 'but on two conditions. First, if it hurts you have to stop. And second, promise we won't go past mother's.'

## Overheard ... at the American juvenile correctional facility

**The bricks:** Outside the correctional facility. When a juvenile is released, he's 'on the bricks'.

**Bug:** A fight.

**Coat party:** A punishment beating. So-called because a coat is thrown over the victim before the beating starts.

**To feen:** To need. As in, 'That guy's really feenin' a coat party.'

**Gladiator school:** A centre renowned for housing the real hard-nuts. So-called because anyone who goes there will end up dead unless they learn to fight.

**To be hooked up:** To be punished by the wardens. Used especially if the screws are deliberately stitching the juvenile up.

**House of pain:** The correction facility.

**Muff:** A push on the face of another juvenile, usually with the intention of goading him in to a bug.

**On the bone:** What you are when you've upset the hardest boys in the centre. As in: 'He shouldn't have told the warden about the bug. He'll be on the bone for months.'

**To peep swiller:** To take a look at the penis of another juvenile in the showers. As in 'Ugh, man – Lionel just peeped swiller.'

**Pressure case:** A weak juvenile; one who easily caves into threats or demands for money.

**Punked out:** How a pressure case is left when he's been squeezed for everything he's got.

**SBO:** Single Bunk Only. An official term used to refer to juveniles who are not allowed to share bunks, usually because they've tried to rape former roommates.

**Woofin':** Make empty threats. As in: 'You ain't gonna cut my throat, man. You just woofin'.'

## **Out for the count**

Depressed, a boxer wanders into a doctor's surgery.

'Doc, you've got to help me,' he moans. 'My insomnia is terrible. I just can't get to sleep at night.'

The doctor peers over his glasses. 'Have you tried counting sheep?' he asks.

The boxer sighs. 'That's no good at all,' he moans. 'Every time I reach nine, I get up.'

## Read all about it!

This gorilla is swinging through the jungle, when he gets to a waterhole and sees a lion bending down having a drink. The gorilla thinks 'I'll have a bit of that', leaps down and shags the lion right up the arse.

Not surprisingly the lion goes beserk. He turns round, roaring savagely. The gorilla shoots off through the jungle with the lion in hot pursuit. Using the branches and creepers to his advantage, the gorilla builds up a bit of a lead and manages to swing into a clearing some 100 yards ahead.

Sitting in the clearing is an old-style hunter with a pith helmet and Don Estelle shorts, leaning back in a deckchair and reading a newspaper. The gorilla whacks him round the head and knocks him out of his chair, before climbing in and hiding behind the newspaper.

The lion comes roaring into the clearing and bounds up to the chair.

'Have you just seen a gorilla?' he asks the figure in the chair.

'What, the one that just fucked a lion up the arse by the waterhole?' replies the gorilla.

'Oh shit,' says the lion. 'It's not in the papers already, is it?'

## Car trouble

A middle-aged lady is in a supermarket when she notices a handsome muscular young man bagging up shopping at one of the checkouts. Making sure she goes through his line, she asks if he'll carry her groceries to her car. 'Sure lady,' he replies cheerfully.

But they're no sooner out of the store, when she beckons him closer. 'You know,' she whispers seductively, 'I have an itchy pussy.'

'You'll have to point it out to me, ma'am. 'All those Japanese cars look alike.'

## Love me, love my dog

Feeling very depressed, a man walks into a pub and orders a triple scotch.
'You know,' says the barman, pouring him the drink. 'That's quite a heavy poison. Is something wrong?'
'Well,' says the man, downing the shots in one. 'I got home and found my wife in bed with my best friend.'
'Wow!' exclaims the bartender. 'No wonder you need a stiff drink – the next one's on the house. So what did you do?'
'I walked over to my wife', the man replies, 'and told her that we were through. I told her to get the hell out.'
'That makes sense', says the bartender, nodding. 'But what about your best friend?'
'Well,' slurs the man, tears in his eyes. 'I walked over to him, looked him right in the eye, and said "Bad dog!"'

## The drums! The drums!

Deep in the Amazonian rain forest, an explorer is leading a party of tourists when the native bearers suddenly pull up at the distant sound of drumming. At the next village, the leader asks one of the local inhabitants to explain the bearers' reaction.
'It's bad,' the local man says, 'very, very bad when the drumming stops.'
Then the man runs off into the forest.
The drumming continues and the now desperate trek leader asks another local man to explain the drumming.
'Oh my God!' the man cries. 'It will be terrible when the drumming stops.'
And this man, too, runs away.
Finally, in terror, the leader grabs a third man and asks him to explain the drumming. As he holds the quaking man, the drumming stops.
'Oh no!' the distressed native cries. 'It's very bad! Now the bass solo starts!'

## Dumb and Dumber

Jim comes home early from work one day, to hear groaning sounds coming from upstairs. Investigating, he finds a bloke in bed humping his wife.
'What the hell's going on here?' he shouts.
His wife turns to her lover, and rolls her eyes.
'See? I told you,' she says, 'He's as thick as pigshit.'

## Tit for tat

Saddam Hussein and George Bush meet up in Baghdad for a round of talks in a new peace process. When George sits down, he notices three buttons on the side of Hussein's chair. They begin talking, and after five minutes Saddam presses the first button. A boxing glove springs out of a box on the desk and punches Bush in the face.

Confused, Bush carries on talking, as Saddam falls about laughing. A few minutes later the second button is pressed, and this time a big boot comes out and kicks Bush in the shin. Again, Hussein laughs, and again Bush carries on talking, not wanting to be put off the bigger issue.

But when the third button is pressed and another boot comes out and kicks Dubya in the balls, he's finally had enough.

'I'm going back home!' he tells the Iraqi. 'We'll finish the talks in two weeks.'

A fortnight passes and Saddam flies to the States for talks. As the two men sit down, Hussein notices three buttons on George's chair and prepares himself for the Yank's revenge. They begin talking and George presses the first button. Saddam ducks, but nothing happens. Bush sniggers.

A few seconds later button two is pressed. Saddam jumps up, but again nothing happens. Bush roars with laughter. When the third button is pressed Saddam jumps up again, and again nothing happens. Bush falls on the floor in a fit of hysterics.

'Sod this,' Saddam says, 'I'm going back to Baghdad.'

'Baghdad?' Bush says through tears of laughter. 'What Baghdad?'

## One down ...

What's the difference between an Australian wedding and an Australian funeral?
One less drunk.

# FHM

## PRESENTS THE BEST OF
## BAR-ROOM JOKES

**THIS IS A CARLTON BOOK**

Text and illustrations copyright © Emap Elan Network 2001
Design copyright © Carlton Books Limited 2001

This edition published by Carlton Books Limited 2001
20 Mortimer Street
London W1T 3JW

A CIP catalogue record for this book is available from the British Library.

ISBN 1 84222 476 X

Editorial Manager: Venetia Penfold
Art Director: Penny Stock
Project Editor: Zia Mattocks
Editor: Sian Parkhouse
Design: DW Design
Illustrations: Nishant Choksi, Griff and David Semple
Production Manager: Garry Lewis

Thanks to *FHM*'s readers for all their jokes

Printed and bound in Great Britain

www.fhm.com/jokes